LUNCHES AND BRUNCHES

Better Homes and Gardens

MEREDITH PRESS

BETTER HOMES AND GARDENS CREATIVE COOKING LIBRARY, FIFTH PRINTING

Contents

This seal means recipe goodness!

Every recipe in this book is *endorsed* by Better Homes & Gardens Test Kitchen. Each food was tested over and over till it rated superior — in practicality, ease of preparation, and deliciousness.

Better Homes *and Gardens*
TEST KITCHEN

Copenhagen Breakfast – wonderful!

← For good company, a grand "Good Morning" — swirly Danish Coffee Ring (page 38), served with ham and mellow cheese, eggs cooked to order, hot coffee. Not enough? Pass Spiced Porridge, fruit.

Lunches

When you entertain the bridge club
at noon or have a few friends in
for luncheon, enjoy your chance to
go all-out on feminine favorites —
which run the gamut from a
spectacular souffle to an unusual
soup-and-sandwich combination.

And for the family, here are hearty,
quick, and make-ahead lunches.
Scan our lunch-box ideas, too (all
sturdy meals — plus a surprise!).
Pick up tips for dieters — pretty
garnishes that add in eye appeal,
easy "low-count" recipes for midday.

Midsummer magic — that's July Jubilee

← For a cooling patio lunch, serve Party Chicken Salad topped
with a "daisy" in full bloom. Trim your salad platter with
bright red Firecracker Plums and refreshing honeydew.

Hot Twist Rolls, made quick from a mix, are a tasty accompaniment. For dessert, offer Strawberry Ice-cream
Meringues. And don't forget sparkling Pink Lemonade —
chill and pretty accompaniment to any summer meal.

Spectacular salad luncheons

Strictly ladylike—these! Whip up a fabulous salad, team it with piping-hot quick bread, cooling dessert and refreshing drink. You're set for a patio party.

```
. . . . . . . . . . . . . . . . . . . . . . . . . . . .

            July Jubilee (page 6)

          Party Chicken Salad
          Firecracker Plums
          Honeydew Wedges
       Twist Rolls      Butter
     Strawberry Ice-cream Meringues
            Pink Lemonade

. . . . . . . . . . . . . . . . . . . . . . . . . . . .
```

Party Chicken Salad

2 cups coarsely diced cooked chicken
2 tablespoons lemon juice
½ teaspoon salt
1 cup sliced celery
1 cup seedless white grapes
2 hard-cooked eggs, chilled and
  chopped
½ cup mayonnaise
¼ cup halved or slivered blanched
  almonds, toasted

Sprinkle chicken with lemon juice and salt; chill several hours. Add celery, grapes, chopped eggs, mayonnaise, and almonds; toss lightly. Season salad with salt to taste. Serve in lettuce-lined bowl. Serves 4 to 5.

Daisy trim: Quarter 2 hard-cooked eggs lengthwise. Remove yolks; sieve. Arrange whites for petals; center with yolks.

Firecracker Plums

1 8-ounce package cream
  cheese, softened
½ cup chopped California walnuts
12 ripe red plums

Combine cream cheese, walnuts, and dash salt. Halve plums; remove pits. Put halves together sandwich-fashion with cheese mixture, letting cheese ruffle out at sides.

Twist Rolls

Prepare plain or rich dough from 1 package hot-roll mix; let rise according to package directions. When ready to shape, roll the dough on lightly floured surface in an 18x6-inch rectangle (about ½ inch thick). Cut in 6-inch strips, ¾ inch wide. Bring both ends of each strip together; pinch ends to seal, then twist strip twice.

Place rolls about 1½ inches apart on greased baking sheet, pressing down on ends. Cover, let rise again according to package directions. Bake at 400° about 12 minutes or till done. Brush tops of warm rolls with butter. Makes 2 dozen.

Strawberry Ice-cream Meringues

Meringue Shells:

3 egg whites
1 teaspoon vanilla
¼ teaspoon cream of tartar
Dash salt
1 cup sugar

• • •

1 pint strawberry ice cream
1 pint strawberries, sliced

Have egg whites at room temperature. Add vanilla, cream of tartar, and salt. Beat till frothy. Gradually add sugar, a small amount at a time, beating till very stiff peaks form and sugar is dissolved.

Cover cooky sheet with plain ungreased paper. Makes 5 large meringue shells, using about ½ cup mixture for each. Shape with spoon to make shells. Bake in very slow oven (275°) 1 hour. For crisper meringues, turn off heat; let dry in oven (door closed) about 1 hour.

Fill cooled Meringue Shells with ice cream; top with sliced strawberries.

Blue-cheese Dip

1 8-ounce package cream cheese
4 ounces blue cheese, crumbled
¼ cup evaporated milk
3 tablespoons chopped pimiento
⅓ cup chopped green pepper
¼ teaspoon garlic salt

Soften cream cheese; add blue cheese; beat till creamy. Stir in remaining ingredients. Chill the dip until ½ hour before serving. Serve with melon balls. Makes 2 cups.

Crab Louis

Louis Dressing:

1 cup mayonnaise or salad dressing
¼ cup whipped cream, whipped
¼ cup chili sauce
¼ cup chopped green pepper
¼ cup chopped green onion and tops
1 teaspoon lemon juice

• • •

1 large head lettuce
2 to 3 cups cooked crab meat, or
    2 6½-ounce cans, chilled
2 large tomatoes, cut in wedges
2 hard-cooked eggs, cut in wedges

Louis Dressing: Combine first 6 ingredients and salt to taste. Chill.

Line four large plates with lettuce. Shred rest of lettuce, arrange on top.

Remove bits of shell from crab. Reserve claw meat; leave remainder in chunks and arrange atop lettuce. Circle with wedges of tomato and egg. Dash with salt. Pour ¼ cup Louis Dressing over each salad. Sprinkle with paprika. Top with claw meat. Pass remaining dressing. Serves 4.

Cheese Bread Sticks

1 package hot-roll mix
1 cup shredded sharp process cheese
1 tablespoon poppy seed

Prepare roll dough according to package directions; add cheese and poppy seed. After dough has risen, divide in half. On lightly floured surface, roll each half to 10x6 inch rectangle. Cut each rectangle in twenty 6-inch-long sticks.

Place on greased cooky sheet. Brush with melted butter. Let rise till double (30 to 45 minutes). Bake in hot oven (400°) 10 minutes or till done. Makes 40.

Marmalade Dessert Pancakes

Sift 1 cup sifted all-purpose flour with 3 teaspoons baking powder. 1 teaspoon sugar, and ¼ teaspoon salt. Beat 1 egg slightly; add 1 cup milk; ¼ cup light cream, and 2 tablespoons melted butter; add flour mixture, beat smooth.

Bake 6-inch cakes on lightly greased griddle. Spread each cake with marmalade, roll up (see below). Keep hot in chafing dish, along with spiced peach halves. Pass Orange-Honey Butter. Makes 10.

Orange-Honey Butter: Cream 1 cup soft butter or margarine. Gradually beat in ½ cup honey. Blend in 1 tablespoon grated orange peel. Mound high in serving bowl. Sprinkle top with grated orange peel.

Use paper towel to roll pancake

Hot Tomato Appetizer

1 No. 2 can (2½ cups) tomato juice
¼ cup *finely* chopped celery
2 tablespoons *finely* chopped
green onions and tops
2 teaspoons soy sauce
1 teaspoon Worcestershire sauce
½ teaspoon curry powder

Combine all ingredients. Salt to taste. Heat through, about 5 minutes. If desired, float thin cucumber slices. Serve hot with crisp crackers. Makes 5 servings.

Chicken in Cheese Shell

1 cup sifted all-purpose flour
¼ teaspoon salt
⅓ cup shortening
⅓ cup shredded sharp process
American cheese
3 to 4 tablespoons cold water

• • •

1½ cups cubed cooked or
canned chicken
1 8¾-ounce can (1 cup) pineapple
tidbits, drained
½ cup chopped California walnuts
½ cup sliced celery
¾ cup dairy sour cream
½ cup mayonnaise

Make a cheese pastry shell of first five ingredients, *adding ¼ cup of cheese* with shortening (save remaining cheese for top). Bake in 8-inch pie plate at 450° for 8 to 10 minutes. Cool. Combine chicken, pineapple, nuts, and celery. Blend sour cream and mayonnaise and add ⅔ *cup* to chicken mixture; mix well. Spoon into pastry shell.

Spread remaining sour-cream mixture over top. Sprinkle with reserved cheese. Chill. Trim with ripe-olive slices. Serves 6.

Pineapple Pickups—in the shell

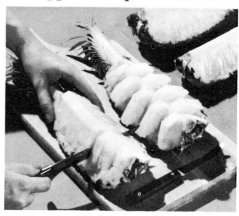

Quarter the pineapple, leaving top on. Cut off core. With grapefruit knife, cut fruit from peel close to the eyes of pineapple.

Slice crosswise. Zigzag by pulling alternate pieces to opposite sides. Serve atop chipped ice; trim with garden flowers or fresh berries.

Curried Chicken Sandwiches

8 slices buttered toast (trim crusts)
8 large slices or 3 cups cubed
cooked chicken
1½ cups salad dressing
⅔ cup finely chopped celery
½ cup sliced green onions and tops
1½ teaspoons curry powder
1 teaspoon salt
Dash pepper

Arrange toast on baking sheet; cover with chicken, sprinkle with salt and pepper. Cut each sandwich in half diagonally. Mix remaining ingredients; spread over chicken to edges of toast. Bake at 375° for 15 minutes. Makes 8 servings.

Bing Cherry Mold

*The top layer is sparkling, clear gelatin; below—
a creamy layer, whipped airy-light and filled
with fresh Bings, crisp almonds—*

> 2 3-ounce packages cherry- or black-
> cherry-flavored gelatin
> 2 cups boiling water
> 1 cup cold water
> 2 teaspoons lemon juice
> 2 tablespoons cooking sherry
>
> • • •
>
> 1 cup dairy sour cream
> 2 cups pitted, halved fresh
> Bing cherries
> ¼ cup chopped blanched
> almonds, toasted

Dissolve gelatin in boiling water; add cold
water and lemon juice. To *1 cup gelatin mixture* add the cooking sherry; pour into a 2-
quart mold and chill till set.

Meanwhile, chill remaining gelatin till
partially set, then whip till fluffy; fold in
sour cream, cherries, and almonds. Pour
atop gelatin layer in mold. Chill till firm,
about 5 hours or overnight.

Unmold on chilled platter. Circle with
fresh Bings, sliced pineapple, romaine.
Pass bowl of sour cream mixed with mayonnaise and sprinkled with toasted almonds. Makes 10 to 12 servings.

Walnut Cream Roll

*It's tender nut cake, rolled around whipped
cream—*

> 4 egg whites
> ½ teaspoon salt
> 1 teaspoon vanilla
> ½ cup sugar
>
> • • •
>
> 4 egg yolks
> ¼ cup sifted all-purpose flour
> ½ cup chopped California walnuts
> 1 cup whipping cream, whipped
> and sweetened

Beat whites with salt and vanilla till soft
peaks form. Gradually beat in sugar, beating till stiff peaks form. Beat yolks till thick
and lemon-colored. Fold yolks into whites;
carefully fold in flour and nuts. Grease and
flour bottom of 15½ x 10½ x 1-inch jellyroll pan. Spread batter evenly in pan.
Bake at 375° for 12 minutes or till cake
springs back when touched.

Immediately loosen sides of cake and
turn out onto towel sprinkled with sifted
confectioners' sugar. Starting at narrow
end, roll cake and towel together; cool on
rack. Unroll; spread with whipped cream.
Reroll cake; chill.

At serving time, top cake roll with
whipped cream and walnut halves if desired. Slice in 8 to 10 servings.

Cooling luncheon salad

Two-toned salad is Bing Cherry Mold—cherry-flavored
gelatin makes both layers. Serve this beauty on a chilled
platter, circled with groups of pineapple slices and Bings.

Salad luncheon tastes as cool as it looks. Ginger Fruit Freeze complements chilled fresh fruits and cheese-ham tidbits.

Minted Iced Tea

Boil 1 quart fresh cold water. Remove from heat; add ⅓ cup tea leaves and 5 mint sprigs. Bruise mint with spoon. Stir well. Let stand uncovered 5 minutes.

Pour 1 quart fresh cold water into a pitcher; strain tea brew into same pitcher. *Don't refrigerate.* At serving time, pour over ice in 10 to 12 tall glasses. Trim with mint.

Midsummer Delight

Ginger Fruit Freeze
Honeydew Wedges with Lime
Pineapple Spears and Berries
Green Grapes
Cheese-Ham Bites
Kona Banana Bread
Lemon Souffle
Minted Iced Tea

Ginger Fruit Freeze

1 3-ounce package cream cheese
3 tablespoons mayonnaise
1 tablespoon lemon juice
¼ teaspoon salt
½ cup chopped preserved kumquats
½ cup dates, cut up
¼ cup quartered maraschino cherries
1 9-ounce can crushed pineapple, drained
2 tablespoons finely chopped candied ginger
1 cup whipping cream, whipped
¼ cup toasted slivered almonds

Soften cream cheese; blend in next 3 ingredients. Sitr in fruits and ginger. Fold in whipped cream. Pour into 1-quart refrigerator tray. Sprinkle with nuts. Freeze firm. Makes 6 to 8 servings.

Kona Banana Bread

Cream ½ cup shortening with 1 cup sugar till light. Add 2 eggs, one at a time, beating well after each. Stir in ¾ cup mashed *ripe* banana. Sift together 1¼ cups sifted cake flour, ¾ teaspoon soda, and ½ teaspoon salt; add to banana mixture. Mix till well blended. Bake in 9x9x2-inch pan at 350° for 30 to 35 minutes. Cut in squares.

Lemon Souffle

6 eggs, separated
½ cup sugar
½ teaspoon grated lemon peel
3 tablespoons lemon juice
Dash salt
½ cup butter or margarine

In top of double boiler, combine beaten egg yolks and all ingredients except egg whites. Cook over *hot, not boiling,* water, stirring constantly, till butter melts and sauce *begins* to thicken (about 4 to 5 minutes). Cool mixture about 15 minutes, beating now and then with electric beater.

Beat egg whites to stiff peaks; gently fold in lemon mixture. Pour into *ungreased* 1½-quart souffle dish or casserole. Set dish in shallow pan, then fill pan to 1 inch with hot water. Bake at 325° for 45 to 50 minutes or till knife inserted comes out clean. Serve at once. Makes 4 to 6 servings.

::::::::::::::::::::::::::::::::::::

Make-ahead Luncheon

Chilled Tomato Juice
Ham Roll-ups   Deviled Eggs
Swiss Cheese
Confetti Relish Mold
Buttered Toasted French Bread
Coconut Ribbon Loaf
Coffee

::::::::::::::::::::::::::::::::::::

Deviled Eggs

6 hard-cooked eggs, halved lengthwise
¼ cup mayonnaise or salad dressing
1 teaspoon vinegar
1 teaspoon prepared mustard
⅛ teaspoon salt
Dash pepper

Remove egg yolks; mash and combine with remaining ingredients. Refill egg whites, using pastry tube if desired. (For plump stuffed eggs, refill only 8 whites; chop extras for salad garnish next day.) Chill.

Note: For extra flavor and color, add one of these to yolk mixture: 2 tablespoons crumbled crisp-cooked bacon—or 1 tablespoon of finely chopped stuffed green or ripe olives—or 1 tablespoon finely chopped green-onion tops or chives.

Confetti Relish Mold

2 beef bouillon cubes
1 3-ounce package lemon-
flavored gelatin
1 cup boiling water
2 tablespoons tarragon vinegar
½ teaspoon salt
1 cup dairy sour cream
½ cup chopped unpared cucumber
¼ cup finely chopped green pepper
¼ cup sliced radishes
2 tablespoons sliced green onions

Dissolve bouillon cubes and gelatin in boiling water. Add vinegar and salt. Chill till mixture is partially set.

Add sour cream, beat smooth. Add remaining ingredients. Pour into a 3-cup mold. Chill till mixture is firm. Serves 6.

Ham Roll-ups

Spread slices of boiled ham with horse-radish and prepared mustard. (Another time, spread with Cheddar process-cheese spread.) Roll up; toothpick to hold.

Coconut Ribbon Loaf

1 10x4x2-inch loaf angel cake
1 pint pink peppermint stick ice cream
1 pint lime sherbet or
pistachio ice cream

• • •

1½ cups whipping cream
1 teaspoon sugar
½ teaspoon vanilla
1 3-ounce can (1¼ cups) flaked
coconut, toasted

Rub brown crumbs off cake. Cut cake lengthwise in three layers. Stir ice cream and sherbet to soften. Spread bottom layer with peppermint-stick ice cream. Add the second cake layer; spread with lime sherbet. Add last cake layer. Place in freezer till ice cream is firm. To serve: Whip cream; stir in sugar and vanilla. Spread over top and sides of loaf. Sprinkle with coconut. Makes 8 to 10 servings.

Tangy Confetti Relish Mold is the star of our luncheon. It's cool, creamy and an excellent accompaniment for ham, eggs, and cheese.

Salad Duet

Perfect Potato Salad
Tomato Aspic
Cold Ham   Relishes
Bacon Cornettes   Butter
Cherry Creme Parfaits
Coffee

Perfect Potato Salad

Sprinkle 5 cups cubed cooked potatoes with 1 teaspoon salt, 2 teaspoons sugar, 1 teaspoon celery seed, and 2 teaspoons vinegar. Add ½ cup chopped onion, 1 cup chopped celery and ½ cup chopped sweet pickle. Add 1½ cups mayonnaise; toss to mix. Fold in 4 hard-cooked eggs, sliced.

Chill well. Serve in center of Tomato Aspic ring. Serve extra in bowl. Serves 8.

Bacon Cornettes

Dice 10 to 12 slices bacon, cook till crisp; drain. Sift together 1 cup sifted all-purpose flour, ¼ cup sugar, 4 teaspoons baking powder, and ¾ teaspoon salt; stir in 1 cup yellow corn meal.

Add 2 eggs, 1 cup milk, and ¼ cup salad oil. Beat just till smooth, about 1 minute (do not overbeat). Stir in bacon. Fill greased muffin pans ⅔ full. Bake at 425° for 20 to 25 minutes. Makes about 1 dozen.

Tomato Aspic

2 envelopes (2 tablespoons) unflavored gelatin
4 cups tomato juice
⅓ cup chopped onion
¼ cup chopped celery leaves
2 tablespoons brown sugar
1 teaspoon salt
2 small bay leaves
4 whole cloves

• • •

3 tablespoons lemon juice
½ to 1 cup finely chopped celery
2 tablespoons chopped green pepper

Soften gelatin in *1 cup* cold tomato juice. Combine *2 cups* of the tomato juice with the next 6 ingredients. Simmer uncovered 5 minutes; strain.

Dissolve the softened gelatin in the *hot* tomato mixture. Add remaining tomato juice and the lemon juice. Chill till partially set. Stir in celery and green pepper. Pour into a 5½-cup ring mold. Chill firm, 5 to 6 hours or overnight. Unmold on chilled platter. Makes 6 to 8 servings.

Cherry Creme Parfaits

Whip 1 cup whipping cream with 3 tablespoons sugar, 1 teaspoon vanilla, and dash salt. Fold in 1 cup dairy sour cream.

Alternate layers of whipped-cream mixture and cherry-pie filling—you'll need one No. 2 can (2½ cups) cherry-pie filling—in parfait or sherbet glasses, beginning with a red layer and ending with a white layer. Top each with a single cherry. Chill till serving time. Serves 8 to 10.

Do you know these Test-Kitchen tips for aspic and potato salad?

To turn out: Loosen edges with tip of knife. Place platter over mold; invert. Wring towel out of hot water; lay over mold. Lift off mold.

The seasonings and vinegar go *directly* on potato slices so the sweet-sour flavors will be absorbed. Add other ingredients; toss.

Sandwich luncheons

When the family is home for lunch, bring on *hearty* sandwiches teamed with soup. (See pages 26-27, too.) for the ladies, it's a *fancy* sandwich plus salad, dessert.

. . . .

Soup and Sandwiches
(*See cover*)

Corned-beef Sandwich Bake
Pickle Fans   Corn Chowder
Lunch-time Salad
Tapioca Pudding   Chilled Milk

. . . .

Corned-beef Sandwich Bake

2 cups packaged biscuit mix
1 12-ounce can corned beef, chilled
2 tablespoons mayonnaise
2 tablespoons prepared mustard
½ cup pitted ripe olives, sliced

• • •

1 large tomato, thinly sliced
4 slices sharp process American
    cheese, halved on diagonal

Prepare biscuit mix according to package directions for rolled biscuits. Roll to 12x7-inch rectangle. Place on ungreased baking sheet. Cut corned beef in 8 slices; arrange in two rows on dough. Mix mayonnaise and mustard; spread over meat. Sprinkle with olives, reserving a few for trim.

Bake at 425° for 15 minutes. Top with tomato slices; dash with pepper. Arrange cheese half-slices atop. Return to oven till cheese melts, about 2 minutes. Top with olive slices. Cut in 8 squares.

Lunch-time Salad

Place lettuce cup on each plate. Fill with torn lettuce and spinach. Drizzle with Italian dressing. Heat frozen onion rings as directed; use as "croutons."

Corn Chowder

5 slices bacon
1 1-pound can whole kernel corn
1 medium onion, thinly sliced
1 cup diced raw pared potatoes
½ teaspoon salt
1 can condensed cream of
    celery soup
1½ cups milk

In large saucepan, cook bacon till crisp. Remove bacon, reserving drippings. Drain corn, reserving liquid. To bacon drippings in saucepan; add reserved liquid, the onion, potatoes, and salt. Cover and simmer 15 minutes or till vegetables are tender. Add soup, milk, and corn; heat through. Season to taste with salt and pepper. Crumble bacon atop. Serves 5 or 6.

. . . .

Spring Medley

Spring Sandwich Puff
Relishes Galore   Potato Chips
Strawberries
to dip in Confectioners' Sugar
Angel Cake Fingers   Coffee

. . . .

Spring Sandwich Puff

In broiler, toast 6 bread slices on one side. Place a slice of process American cheese on each untoasted side; broil to partially melt cheese. Remove from heat, and place 3 or 4 spears of hot cooked asparagus on top of each cheese slice.

Beat 3 egg yolks till thick and lemon-colored, stir in ¼ cup mayonnaise, ¼ teaspoon salt, and dash pepper; fold in 3 stiff-beaten egg whites. Pile mixture atop asparagus. Bake at 350° about 13 minutes or till egg mixture is set. Serves 6.

Spring Sandwich Puffs— These high-hat cheese sandwiches are strictly company. Tops are like little souffles, so rush these straight to the table. Serve relishes (let celery leaves be trim).

Sure to be a hit at the club luncheon is Tomato Soup with Avocado. Offer crackers *or* toast fingers with cheese broiled atop.

Tomato Soup with Avocado

Avocado slices make this soup extra special—

Combine 1 can tomato soup, 1 soup-can water, 1 can beef broth, ¼ teaspoon crushed oregano, and ⅛ teaspoon garlic powder. Heat to boiling, reduce heat, simmer 5 minutes. Pour into 4 bowls; float 2 thin slices avocado atop each serving.

Luncheon for Three Ladies

Hot Ham and Asparagus Sandwich
Olives   Carrot Sticks
Orange Sections with Coconut
Spiced Iced Tea

Bridge Club Luncheon

Tomato Soup with Avocado
Crackers   Club Sandwiches
Lime Sherbet   Ladyfingers
Hot Coffee

Club Sandwiches

8 slices enriched white bread
½ cup mayonnaise seasoned with
   ½ teaspoon curry powder
8 slices Bologna
1 medium cucumber, unpeeled, sliced
8 slices process Swiss cheese
Prepared mustard
Leaf lettuce
4 slices whole-wheat bread

Trim crusts from bread, if desired. Spread white bread with curried mayonnaise.

On 4 slices, stack *half* the Bologna, cucumber, and cheese. Spread cheese with mustard; top with lettuce, whole-wheat bread. Spread with curried mayonnaise; stack remaining fillings, lettuce, bread. Quarter sandwiches. Peg each quarter with an olive-topped toothpick. Makes 4.

Hot Ham and Asparagus Sandwich

3 slices buttered toast, halved
   diagonally
3 slices boiled ham, halved diagonally
1 10-ounce package frozen asparagus
   spears, cooked and drained
Cheese Sauce

In 3 individual casseroles, place toast, two half-slices to a casserole, cut edges down. Top with ham, then bundles of hot asparagus. Ladle hot Cheese Sauce over.

Cheese Sauce: Make white sauce of 1 tablespoon butter, 1½ teaspoons all-purpose flour, dash salt and pepper, and ½ cup milk. Add ½ cup shredded process American cheese and stir till melted.

Spiced Iced Tea

Measure 3 tablespoons tea into pot. Pour in 2 cups boiling water; add 3 inches stick cinnamon and 1 teaspoon whole cloves tied in bag. Cover, steep 5 minutes; stir.

Strain tea into pitcher; return spices to tea. At once add 2 cups cold water; cool to room temperature. Remove spices; stir in ½ cup orange juice, ¼ cup sugar. Chill. Pour over ice. Makes 4½ cups tea.

Vegetables for variety

Vegetable-Deviled Ham Casserole

1 10-ounce package frozen corn
1 10-ounce package frozen baby Limas
1 cup dairy sour cream
1 4½-ounce can deviled ham
2 tablespoons minced onion
¼ teaspoon salt
1 3-ounce can (⅔ cup) broiled
  sliced mushrooms, drained
½ cup fresh bread crumbs, combined
  with 1 tablespoon butter, melted

Cook frozen vegetables according to package directions. Drain. Mix vegetables with next 5 ingredients. Turn into 10x6x1½-inch baking dish. Top with buttered bread crumbs; sprinkle with paprika. Bake in moderate oven (350°) for 25 to 30 minutes or until hot. Makes 6 servings.

Apple-Grapefruit Mold

1 1-pound can (2 cups) grapefruit
2 3-ounce packages lime-flavored
  gelatin
2 cups boiling water
1½ cups diced unpared apple
¼ cup broken California walnuts

Drain grapefruit, reserving juice; cut up grapefruit. Dissolve gelatin in boiling water. Add grapefruit juice, plus enough water to make 2 cups. Chill till slightly thick.
   Add apple, grapefruit, and nuts. Pour into 5½ cup mold. Chill till set. Unmold; trim with walnut halves. Serves 8.

Herbed Spinach Bake

1 10-ounce package frozen spinach,
  cooked and drained
1 cup cooked rice
1 cup shredded sharp process cheese
2 slightly beaten eggs
2 tablespoons soft butter or margarine
⅓ cup milk
2 tablespoons chopped onion
½ teaspoon Worcestershire sauce
1 teaspoon salt
¼ teaspoon rosemary, crushed

Combine ingredients. Pour into 10x6x1½-inch baking dish. Bake in moderate oven (350°) for 20 to 25 minutes or till knife inserted between center and edge comes out clean. Cut in 6 squares.

Carrot-stick Bundles

Thread several carrot matchsticks through a pitted ripe olive. Allow 2 "bundles" per person. Serve chilled.

Banana Brittle Dessert

2 fully ripe bananas
¾ cup crushed peanut brittle
1 teaspoon vanilla
1 cup whipping cream, whipped

Peel bananas; slice thinly. Fold banana, peanut brittle, and vanilla into whipped cream. Spoon into 4 sherbets. Chill 1 hour. Top with more crushed peanut brittle.

Star a swank souffle

High-hat Cheese Souffle

¼ cup butter or margarine
¼ cup all-purpose flour
½ teaspoon salt
Dash cayenne
1 cup milk
½ pound sharp process American
   cheese, thinly sliced
4 egg yolks
4 stiff-beaten egg whites

Melt butter; blend in the flour, salt and cayenne. Add milk; cook quickly, stirring constantly, till mixture thickens and bubbles. Add cheese; stir till cheese melts. Remove mixture from heat.

Beat egg yolks till thick and lemon-colored. Slowly add cheese mixture to egg yolks, stirring constantly. Cool mixture slightly, then pour slowly into beaten egg whites, folding together thoroughly.

Pour mixture into ungreased 1½-quart souffle dish or casserole. For a top hat (it puffs in the oven!) trace a circle through mixture 1 inch from edge and 1 inch deep. Bake at 300° for 1 hour and 15 minutes or till knife comes out clean.

Bake an airy cheese souffle—

← Billowy and light as a cloud—this souffle's the kind you dream about. It's topped with a golden crown, and whiffs of the tangy sharp-cheese goodness inside. A masterpiece!

French Green Salad

1 clove garlic, cut
½ teaspoon salt
¼ teaspoon dry mustard
¼ teaspoon paprika
Fresh-ground pepper
¼ cup salad oil
      • • •
4 cups greens, any combination
2 tablespoons vinegar
2 tablespoons lemon juice

Rub salad bowl with garlic. Measure in salt, mustard, and paprika. Grind pepper over; blend. Beat in salad oil with a fork.

Add greens. Toss till leaves glisten. Sprinkle with vinegar and lemon juice. Complete tossing. Makes 4 to 6 servings.

Pots de Creme

1 6-ounce package (1 cup)
   semisweet chocolate pieces
1¼ cups light cream
      • • •
2 egg yolks
Dash salt

In heavy saucepan, combine chocolate pieces and cream. Stir over low heat till blended and *satin-smooth*. Mixture should be *slightly thick* — but don't let it boil. Beat egg yolks with salt till thick and light. Gradually stir in chocolate mixture.

Spoon mixture into 6 or 7 traditional cups or into small sherbets, filling ⅔ full. Cover and chill at least 3 hours or till mixture is consistency of pudding.

Demitasse

Use 3 to 4 tablespoons coffee to 1 measuring cup water. Use any desired method. Serve hot in small cups, usually black, with or without sugar.

To make six ⅓-cup servings—instantly, measure 3 tablespoons instant coffee (more or less to suit your taste) into your coffee server. Stir in 2 cups boiling water.

Hearty midday meals

When lunch is the big meal or friends are coming for lunch-and-bridge, line up a quick casserole, simple salad, and make-ahead dessert—cooking's done in no time.

Easy Chicken Chow Mein

2 cups diced cooked or
   canned chicken or turkey
1 can condensed cream of
   mushroom soup
1 9-ounce can (1 cup)
   pineapple tidbits
1 tablespoon soy sauce
1 cup celery slices
2 tablespoons chopped green onions
1 3-ounce can (2½ cups) chow-mein
   noodles

Combine all ingredients except noodles, mixing well. Gently fold in *1 cup of the noodles*. Turn into 8x8x2-inch baking dish. Sprinkle with remaining noodles. Bake in moderate oven (350°) 50 minutes or till hot. Makes 4 or 5 servings. Pass soy sauce.

Avocado-Cranberry Salad

Another quickie—avocado slices and tomato—

Arrange avocado halves or quarters on lettuce. Top with mixture of cubed canned jellied cranberry sauce and diced celery. Serve with French dressing.

Coconut-Oatmeal Cookies

2 cups quick-cooking rolled oats
⅔ cup flaked coconut
1 cup butter or margarine
1 cup sugar
2 eggs
3 tablespoons milk
1½ teaspoons vanilla
1½ cups sifted all-purpose flour
½ teaspoon *each* soda and salt

In oven, toast oats and coconut till golden brown. Thoroughly cream butter and sugar; add eggs, milk, and vanilla, beating well. Sift together dry ingredients; add to creamed mixture, blending well. Stir in oats and coconut.

Drop from teaspoon, 2 inches apart, on ungreased cooky sheet. Flatten with a tumbler dipped in sugar. If desired, sprinkle tops with untoasted coconut. Bake in a hot oven (400°) 8 to 10 minutes or till lightly browned. Remove at once from pan; cool. Makes 4 dozen.

Caramel Crunch

In skillet, toast ½ cup coarsely broken pecans in 2 tablespoons butter, stirring often. Add ½ cup tiny caramel or butterscotch pieces; heat and stir until melted. Cool to room temperature.

Stir 1 quart vanilla ice cream just to soften. To "chip," dot with caramel mixture over ice cream, fold in. Turn into refrigerator tray. Freeze. Makes 1 quart.

Homespun and so easy— Start with the canned foods on your shelves and come up with tasty dishes like these. Western Chili Casserole is "family-spiced," will become a favorite.

Western Chili Casserole

1 pound ground beef
1 cup chopped onion
¼ cup chopped celery
1 15-ounce can chili con carne
  with beans
¼ teaspoon pepper
2 cups corn chips, slightly crushed
1 cup shredded, sharp process cheese

Brown meat; add ¾ *cup* of onion and the celery; cook till just tender. *Drain off excess fat.* Add chili and pepper; heat. Place layer of chips in ungreased 1½-quart casserole. Alternate layers of chili mixture, chips, and cheese, reserving ½ cup chips and ¼ cup cheese for trim. Sprinkle center with reserved cheese and onion.

Cover and bake at 350° for 10 minutes or till hot through. To serve, border casserole with corn chips. Makes 6 servings.

Beet and Bean Salad

Combine ½ cup clear French Dressing, ¼ cup minced onion, ½ teaspoon dry mustard, ¼ teaspoon *each* salt and rosemary, dash pepper. Drain one 1-pound can whole green beans; pour dressing over beans. Chill several hours, spooning dressing over beans often. Drain.

Arrange one 1-pint jar sliced pickled beets on leaf lettuce, top with beans.

Corn-bread Sticks

For speed, make corn bread and use a mix—

1 cup sifted all-purpose flour
¼ cup sugar
4 teaspoons baking powder
¾ teaspoon salt
1 cup yellow corn meal
2 eggs
1 cup milk
¼ cup soft shortening

Sift flour with sugar, baking powder, and salt; stir in corn meal. Add eggs, milk, and shortening. Beat with rotary or electric beater till just smooth, about 1 minute. (Do not overbeat.) Spoon batter into greased corn-stick pans, filling ⅔ full. Bake at 425° for 12 to 15 minutes.

Double-easy Fruit Dessert

Whip this up after breakfast. It's ready to serve for lunch—

1 No. 2½ can (3½ cups) fruits for
  salad, well drained
1 cup tiny marshmallows
1 cup dairy sour cream
1 tablespoon lemon juice
1 tablespoon sugar
¼ teaspoon salt

Mix all ingredients and chill several hours. Top with maraschino cherries. Serves 5 or 6.

Cheese Fan's Choice

Three-cheese Lasagne
Crisp Bread Sticks
Cucumber Fingers and Carrot Strips
Cauliflowerets
Fresh Berries with Cream *or* Apples
Cinnamon Crisp Cookies   Milk

Lenten Special

Fiesta Salmon or Tuna Bake
Lemon Wedges
Buttered Green Beans
Toasted English Muffins
"Frosted" Pineapple Squares
Coffee

Three-cheese Lasagne

6 ounces (about 3½ cups) wide noodles
1 1½-ounce envelope
   spaghetti-sauce mix
1 6-ounce can (⅔ cup)
   tomato paste
1 beaten egg
1½ cups large-curd, cream-style
   cottage cheese
1 teaspoon salt
1 6- or 8-ounce package sliced
   Mozzarella cheese
¼ cup grated Parmesan cheese

Cook noodles in boiling salted water till tender; drain. Prepare spaghetti-sauce mix according to package directions, using the tomato paste. Combine egg, cottage cheese, and salt; mix well.

In greased 10x6x1½-inch baking dish, alternate layers of *half* each of the noodles, sauce, cottage cheese, Mozzarella, and Parmesan. Repeat layers. Bake in moderate oven (375°) 30 minutes. Let stand 15 minutes before serving. Makes 6 servings.

Cinnamon Crisp Cookies

Thoroughly cream ½ cup butter and 1 cup brown sugar. Beat in 1 egg and 1 tablespoon shredded orange peel. Sift together 1½ cups sifted all-purpose flour, 1 teaspoon baking powder, 1 teaspoon cinnamon, and ¼ teaspoon salt; add to creamed mixture. Stir in ½ cup bran flakes and ¼ cup chopped pecans. Chill 1 hour.

Shape in 2 long 1½-inch rolls. Wrap in waxed paper; chill well. Slice ⅛ to ¼ inch thick. Bake on greased cooky sheet at 350° for 8 to 10 minutes. Makes 4 dozen.

Fiesta Salmon or Tuna Bake

4 hard-cooked eggs
2 tablespoons mayonnaise
¼ teaspoon *each* salt, dry mustard
Dash bottled hot pepper sauce
1 1-pound can salmon *or* 2 6½- or
   7-ounce cans tuna, drained
1 teaspoon lemon juice
¼ cup butter or margarine
¼ cup flour
½ teaspoon salt
2 cups milk
¾ cup shredded process cheese
About 12 pitted ripe olives
1 cup crushed potato chips

Make deviled eggs of first 5 ingredients. Break fish in chunks; line 10x6x1½-inch baking dish; sprinkle with lemon juice.

Melt butter; blend in flour and salt; stir in milk; cook and stir till thickened. Stir in cheese. Pour *half* of cheese sauce over fish. Arrange deviled eggs and olives atop. *Cover* with remaining sauce. Sprinkle with potato chips. Bake at 375° for 25 minutes or till hot. Makes 5 or 6 servings.

"Frosted" Pineapple Squares

1 No. 2 can pineapple tidbits
1 3-ounce package lime-
   flavored gelatin
2 cups tiny marshmallows
1 cup whipping cream, whipped

Drain pineapple, reserving syrup. Add water to syrup to make 2 cups; heat to boiling; add gelatin and stir to dissolve.

Add pineapple; pour into 10x6x1½-inch baking dish. Cover immediately with a layer of marshmallows. Spread top with whipped cream; chill. Cut in 8 squares.

When friends come for lunch, and you want to fuss a bit—

Turn out wonderful Chicken Croquettes. They boast hot creamy-soft interiors, crunchy jackets. You may have forgotten just how good they are!

Serve topped with *Green Peas in Cream Sauce:* Melt 2 tablespoons butter; blend in 2 tablespoons all-purpose flour. Add ½ cup light cream and ½ cup chicken broth all at once. Cook and stir till mixture thickens and bubbles. Add ¼ teaspoon salt, dash pepper, and ½ cup drained cooked or canned peas. Heat through. Spoon over croquettes just before serving.

Strawberry Sherbet

4 cups fresh ripe strawberries

• • •

2 cups sugar
2 cups buttermilk

Rinse, drain, and hull strawberries. Add sugar to berries, and mash. Stir in buttermilk. Pour into refrigerator trays; freeze.

Break in chunks; beat with electric beater till smooth.* Freeze firm. Makes 10 servings. Sentimental trim: Top each serving with a candied violet.

*Or partially freeze; then beat with rotary beater. Freeze firm.

Chicken Croquettes

3 tablespoons butter or margarine
¼ cup all-purpose flour
½ cup milk
½ cup chicken broth
1 tablespoon minced parsley
1 teaspoon lemon juice
1 teaspoon grated onion
Dash *each* paprika, pepper, and
    nutmeg
¼ teaspoon salt
1½ cups finely diced cooked or
    canned chicken

• • •

¾ cup fine dry bread crumbs
1 beaten egg
2 tablespoons water

Melt butter; blend in flour; add milk and broth. Cook and stir till mixture bubbles; cook and stir 1 minute longer. Add parsley, lemon juice, onion, and seasonings. Cool. Add chicken, salt to taste; chill.

With wet hands, shape chicken mixture in 8 balls, a scant ¼ cup each. Roll in crumbs. Shape balls into cones, handling lightly so crumbs remain on outside. Dip into mixture of egg and water; roll in crumbs again. Fry in deep hot fat (365°) 2½ to 3 minutes or till golden brown and hot through. Drain on paper towels; serve with Green Peas in Cream Sauce. Serves 4.

Lunch-box favorites

Packing a delicious lunch is a snap today. Look over your grocer's shelves for exciting, ready-to-travel foods. You'll find breads by the dozen, fillings in can or jar, cheese and crackers in tiny packages.

Remember canned soup to send along in a vacuum bottle—makes an appetizing "something hot." Or let a wide-mouth vacuum tote main-dish fare—hot *or* cold. Dessert: packaged cake, cookies, jellyroll.

Tips for sandwich makers

• If you use frozen bread, the slices won't tear in spreading.
• Make a week's supply of sandwiches at once—bank them in your freezer (always at 0°). Pack them while still frozen—they'll be just right for lunch.
• These sandwich fillings freeze best: peanut butter, chicken, and meat.

Big Meal for a Big Appetite

Hot Vegetable Soup
or
Beef Stew
Corned Beef on Rye
Pickles   Coleslaw
Cherry Pie
Tomato Juice
Snack: Cheese and Crackers

The First Grades

Chicken Drumstick
Bread-and-Butter Sandwiches
Carrot Sticks   Leafy Lettuce
Cherry Tomatoes
Jumbo Sugar Cooky
Hot Cocoa
with Miniature Marshmallows
Snack: Apple or Popcorn Ball

Kid's Delight

Peanut Butter-Bacon Sandwich
Cream of Tomato Soup
Carrot-Raisin Salad
Oatmeal Cooky
Cold Milk
Snack: Big bunch of grapes

Executive on a Diet

Hot Consomme
(sparked with bay leaf and thyme)
Cold Turkey Slices
Hard-cooked Egg Crisp Rye Wafers
Lettuce with Low-calorie Dressing
Ripe, Juicy Tomato
Hot Black Tea
Snack: Giant Orange

Styled For Career Girl

Chilled Sliced Fruit
Cottage Cheese
Finger Sandwiches filled
with Deviled Ham
Fresh Ripe Pear
Jellyroll Slice
Cold Milk
Snack: Bunch of Grapes

"In" for Teens

Submarine Sandwich
(Pack fillings separately—meat,
cheese, lettuce, and mustard)
Dill Pickle   Fresh Fruit, Raisins
Chocolate Milk
Snack: Cupcake, Grape Juice

Remember these ideas when packing lunches.
Add fun and good eating to "carry" meals—

Pack sandwich and lettuce (also salad and dressing) separately so lettuce stays crisp. Put together just before eating.

To pack a fruit-cottage cheese salad, put fruit in wide-mouth vacuum bottle. Make a "sling" of clear plastic wrap for cottage cheese and place it atop the fruit. Wrap lettuce separately. Pack a cupcake inside a paper cup, so frosting stays on.

Sometimes, tuck in a chicken drumstick (coat with seasoned flour, not batter, so coating stays crisp).

Peel and halve a hard-cooked egg for easy eating later. "Start" the peel on an orange (cut peel in sections; pull back one end of each), wrap in clear plastic wrap—it will be easier to eat.

Freeze a can of juice to add to lunch box; it will thaw by lunch time. Another chiller: Canned ice. When cocoa's the drink, send a packet of tiny marshmallows to float atop.

Low-calorie lunches

When you're watching your calorie intake, planned meals are a big help in avoiding temptation. Here are 8 sample lunches that "weigh in" at under 500 calories each.

Cheese-stuffed Frank

Split 1 frankfurter lengthwise, not quite through bottom. Combine ¼ cup instant mashed potatoes and 1 tablespoon grated Parmesan cheese. Fill frankfurter. Sprinkle additional Parmesan cheese atop potatoes. Place on baking sheet; heat in 400° oven for 8 to 10 minutes. Serve hot. *232 calories*.

Citrus Salad

Line a salad plate with 2 large lettuce leaves. Atop, arrange ½ orange in sections and ¼ grapefruit in sections. *65 calories*.

Green Salad

Rub cut end of garlic clove inside individual salad bowls. Break lettuce into bowls by hand, in bite-size pieces—it looks fresher than lettuce cut with a knife.

For a treat, try different greens—Bibb lettuce, water cress, escarole, or spinach.

Season. Tuck in tomato wedges (½ tomato per bowl). *Salad rates 35 calories per 1-cup serving without dressing*. Drizzle salads with bottled blue-cheese dressing, or use Tomato Dressing (see opposite page).

Egg-Onion Salad

Line a chilled plate with 2 large lettuce leaves. Alternate slices of one hard-cooked egg and rings of one onion slice. *90 calories*. Top with low-calorie dressing.

Speedy Frankfurter Lunch

Cheese-stuffed Frank (recipe above)
Dill Pickle Slices
(1 large pickle cut in slices)
Celery Curls (3 stalks)
Carrot Sticks (½ medium carrot)
Chocolate Pudding
(½ cup low-calorie)
Cold Milk (1 cup skim)

Slim-trim Luncheon

Hot Tomato Juice (1 cup)
Pan-fried Baby-beef Liver
(2 ounces)
Cauliflowerets (cooked, ½ cup)
Butter (½ tablespoon)
Citrus Salad (recipe above)
Angel Cake (2-inch wedge)
Buttermilk (1 cup)

Easy Fish Fare

Fish Sticks (2)   Lemon Wedge (1)
Green Salad (1 cup, recipe above)
Blue-cheese Dressing
(1 tablespoon low-calorie)
Rye Bread (1 slice)   Butter (1 pat)
Orange Sherbet (½ cup)
Sugar Wafers (2)
Chilled Milk (1 cup skim)

Soup-and-salad Lunch

Vegetable-Beef Soup (1 cup)
Egg-Onion Salad (recipe above)
Salad Dressing
(1 tablespoon low-calorie)
Hard Roll (1 medium)
Butter or Margarine (½ tablespoon)
Prune Plums (½ cup dietetic-pack)
Cold Milk (1 cup skim)

Cantaloupe Stars

Stand a large cantaloupe on end. To halve melon so the edge looks like giant rickrack braid, thrust a sharp knife into the center at an angle; pull it out and make the next cut at the opposite angle. (See picture.) Repeat around melon and pull the halves apart. Remove seeds.

Fill the centers with a mixture of fresh fruits — strawberries, raspberries, pitted cherries or grapes, melon balls or pineapple chunks. Now drizzle thawed frozen lemonade concentrate (undiluted) over the fruit. Chill until serving time. One cantaloupe makes 2 servings.

Tomato Dressing

In a jar, combine one 8-ounce can seasoned tomato sauce, 2 tablespoons tarragon vinegar, 1 teaspoon onion juice, 1 teaspoon Worcestershire sauce, and ½ teaspoon *each* salt, dill seed, and basil. Shake. Chill. *Calories per tablespoon: 5.*

Showmanship goes a long way when you're counting calories. Attractive garnishes like mint sprigs, lemon slices, and paprika add in the form of eye appeal, not in calories.

Cheeseburger Lunch

Cheeseburger
(¼ pound patty of lean ground beef,
one 1-ounce slice American cheese,
one slice toasted white bread)
Dill Pickle (1 medium)
Orange-flavored Gelatin
(½ cup low-calorie)
Tea or Coffee

Raid-the-refrigerator Lunch

Sandwich of:
Chilled Meatloaf (2 ounces)
Whole-wheat Bread (2 slices)
Tomato (2 slices)
Butter or Margarine (1 pat)
Hard-cooked Egg (1 egg, sliced)
Fruit Cocktail (½ cup dietetic-pack)
Milk (1 cup skim)

Think-thin Luncheon

Beef Broth (1 cup)
Fruit-Cheese Plate of:
Orange Sections (½ orange)
Grapefruit Sections (½ grapefruit)
Grapes (1 cup)
Cottage Cheese (½ cup)
Cracked Wheat Bread (1 slice)
Butter (½ tablespoon)
Milk (1 cup skim)

Cold Plate Special

Tomato Juice (1 cup)
Cocktail Crackers (2)
Cold Plate of:
Shrimp (5 medium)
Shrimp Cocktail Sauce (1 tablespoon)
Deviled Eggs (2 halves)
Radishes (4)
Sliced Peaches (1 cup dietetic-pack)
Chilled Milk (1 cup skim)

Brunches

Just the ticket for friendly
light entertaining—whether you're
enjoying weekend guests, chairing
a club "event," or celebrating a
birthday or engagement. Brunch is
a dandy family idea, too—especially
on "big-dinner" holidays.

Go as homey as eggs and bacon,
with fruit the fancy touch—or as
elegant as creamed sweetbreads in
flaky patty shells. Above all,
plan on easy hostessing. Serve,
pour steaming cups of coffee, and
settle back to enjoy the "top of
the morning" with your guests.

Exquisite—Brunch Boutique, a la Paris—

← Eggs, Eiffel Tower, fairly billow out of dainty ramekins.
Serve with whole strawberries or Breakfast Salad, and
Croissants with butter curls. Or offer frizzled ham slices and
berry-topped Toast Blintzes. Pour Cafe au Lait (use two
pitchers) or pass French Chocolate. Finale: Serve baby
radishes to spread with butter—they're quite delicious!

The all-out brunch

When brunch is a celebration, bring out the sterling and fine china, the thin-stemmed sherbets, and the lace-edged napkins. The foods – fancy, of course!

Brunch Boutique

Iced Tomato Cocktail
Eggs, Eiffel Tower
Frizzled Ham Slices
Toast Blintzes with Strawberries
Coffee
Crisp Radishes with Butter

Iced Tomato Cocktail

Combine two parts chilled tomato juice and one part sauerkraut juice. Pour over crushed ice in cocktail glasses.

Toast Blintzes

16 slices enriched sandwich bread
3 tablespoons milk
1 cup drained large-curd cream-style
   cottage cheese
3 tablespoons butter or
   margarine, melted
   • • •
2 cups sweetened sliced strawberries
   or 2 10-ounce packages frozen

Cut 3-inch rounds from bread, using a cooky cutter. Brush the top edge of all bread rounds with milk. Place 2 table-spoons cottage cheese in center of each of 8 rounds. Place a plain round, milk-brushed side down, over cheese; press edges together.

Brush tops with melted butter. Toast on a baking sheet in hot oven (400°) about 10 minutes or until golden brown. Serve hot with strawberries to spoon over. Makes 8 Blintzes or 4 servings.

Eggs, Eiffel Tower

4 rusks or slices dry toast
1 4½-ounce can deviled ham
¾ cup shredded process cheese
6 egg whites
¼ teaspoon cream of tartar
10 drops bottled hot pepper sauce
Dash salt
1 teaspoon prepared mustard
6 egg yolks

Cut rusks or toast in rounds to fit in bottom of 4 ramekins or 6-ounce custard cups. Butter each rusk; spread with 1 tablespoon deviled ham, place in ramekin and sprinkle with 1 tablespoon cheese.

Beat egg whites with cream of tartar, hot pepper sauce, and salt till soft peaks form; gradually add mustard, beating till stiff peaks form. Place heaping tablespoon of egg-white mixture on top of cheese in each ramekin. Top with egg yolks (place 2 yolks in 2 of the ramekins). Dot layer with bits of deviled ham (about ½ tablespoon on each) and sprinkle with 1 tablespoon cheese. Top with egg-white mixture.

Repeat layers of ham, cheese, and egg white, building up a peak of egg-white mixture. (See picture, page 30.)

Bake in slow oven (325°) about 30 minutes, or till golden and yolks are of desired doneness. Makes 4 servings.

Blue-ribbon Brunch

Mock Pink Champagne
Western Shrimp Supreme
Tiny Buttered Biscuits
Green and Gold Salad with
Chutney Dressing
Plum Melange
Coffee Cake*   Butter Balls
Demitasse
*See pages 56-59

Mock Pink Champagne

½ cup sugar
1 cup water
1 cup grapefruit juice
½ cup orange juice
¼ cup grenadine syrup
1 1-pint 12-ounce bottle
   ginger ale, chilled
Twists of lemon peel
Stems-on maraschino cherries

Combine sugar and water in saucepan; simmer uncovered, stirring constantly, till sugar is dissolved, about 3 minutes. Cool.

Mix with fruit juices and grenadine syrup in punch bowl. Chill.

Just before serving, add ginger ale, pouring it slowly down side of bowl. Serve over ice in sherbet glasses. Trim each with peel and a cherry. Makes 6½ cups.

Western Shrimp Supreme

1 cup sliced fresh mushrooms
2 tablespoons butter
2 tablespoons all-purpose flour
½ cup light cream
1 can condensed cream of
   mushroom soup
⅓ cup cooking sherry
3 tablespoons grated Parmesan cheese
2 7-ounce packages frozen
   shelled shrimp, cooked
1 15-ounce can artichoke hearts,
   drained and halved
¼ cup toasted slivered blanched
   almonds

Cook mushrooms in butter till tender. Push to one side in skillet; blend in flour. Gradually stir in cream. Bring to boil and cook and stir 1 minute. Blend in soup, sherry, and cheese. Stir in shrimp and artichokes. Heat through, stirring gently.

Transfer to chafing dish to keep warm. Sprinkle almonds atop. Add fluff of water cress. Serve over tiny hot buttered biscuits or patty shells. Makes 6 servings.

Green and Gold Salad

Line individual salad plates with leaf lettuce. Fan several chilled canned pineapple spears on each. Tuck in lemon-juice-sprinkled avocado slices between. Add a jaunty flag of water cress at top of fan. Spoon Chutney Dressing across fruits.

Chutney Dressing

In jar, combine one 8½-ounce bottle chutney, finely snipped, ¾ cup salad oil, ¼ cup vinegar, and 1 teaspoon *each* sugar and salt. Cover; shake well. Chill. Shake again just before serving. Makes 2 cups.

Plum Melange

1 No. 2½ can (3½ cups)
   greengage plums
2 teaspoons cornstarch
2 tablespoons julienne strips of
   candied ginger
1 No. 2½ can (3½ cups) purple
   plums, drained
Dairy sour cream

Drain greengage plums, reserving syrup. In saucepan, blend reserved syrup and cornstarch. Add candied ginger. Cook and stir till mixture thickens and comes to a boil. Cool to warm, about 30 minutes.

Arrange all plums in serving bowl. Pour ginger syrup over. Chill. Serve with sour cream. Makes 6 servings.

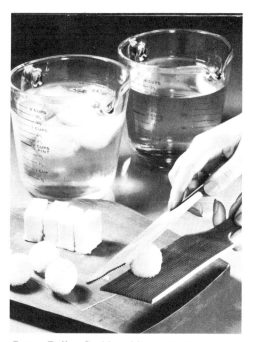

Butter Balls — Scald paddles in boiling water; chill in ice water. Cut firm butter in ½-inch pats. Hold bottom paddle still; move top paddle round. If butter clings to paddle, dip again in hot water, then in icy water.

Easter Morning

Berry-Grapefruit Cup
Cheese-filled Omelet
Ham   Brown-and-serve Sausages
Fruited Hot Cross Buns
Butter Balls   Jams   Marmalade
Steaming Coffee

Cheese-filled Omelet

8 egg yolks
¼ cup all-purpose flour
Dash pepper
8 egg whites
¼ cup water
1 teaspoon salt
1 recipe Cheese Sauce*

Combine egg yolks, flour, and a dash pepper; beat till *very thick*. Beat whites till frothy; add water and salt; beat till stiff but not dry. Fold yolk mixture into whites, gently but thoroughly.

Pile into 2 *well-greased, hot* 8½x1¾-inch round ovenware cake dishes. Bake at 350° for 15 minutes, or till done.

Put omelets together, layer-cake style, with Cheese Sauce between and on top. Serve at once, cutting into pie-shaped wedges with two forks. Makes 6 servings.

*If you're in a hurry, simply melt one 8-ounce jar triple-use cheese spread.

Cheese Sauce

2 tablespoons butter or margarine
2 tablespoons all-purpose flour
¼ teaspoon salt
1 cup milk
1 cup shredded sharp Cheddar cheese

Melt butter, blend in flour and salt. Add milk; cook and stir till thickened. Add cheese. Stir till melted. Makes 1½ cups.

Easter breakfast, all decked out

First, a refreshing fruit cup. Then comes the dramatic omelet — with ham, sausage, and Easter-special Hot Cross Buns. Favors might be bright eggs and posies in parsley baskets.

Fruited Hot Cross Buns

1 package hot-roll mix
2 tablespoons soft butter
2 tablespoons golden seedless raisins
2 tablespoons chopped mixed
   candied fruits and peels
⅓ cup sugar
1 teaspoon cinnamon
½ teaspoon nutmeg
1 slightly beaten egg

Prepare roll mix according to package directions; add butter and fruits to liquid mixture and sugar and spices to dry ingredients. Mix well.

Cover and let rise in warm place till double (about 1½ hours). Turn out on lightly floured surface and knead till smooth. Shape 16 buns; place on greased baking sheet. Cover and let rise till almost double (about 50 minutes). Brush tops with egg mixed with 1 tablespoon water.

Bake at 375° for 15 minutes or till done. Cool slightly; make crosses with Confectioners' Icing. Serve warm.

Confectioners' Icing: Add enough milk or cream to 1 cup sifted confectioners' sugar to make of spreading consistency. Add dash salt and ½ teaspoon vanilla.

Especially for Christmas

Hot Cranberry Juice Cocktail
Creamed Sweetbreads in
Patty Shells
Marinated Artichoke Hearts
Cantaloupe Pickles
Fruitcake   Christmas Cookies
Coffee

Marinated Artichoke Hearts

1 package frozen artichoke hearts
2 tablespoons lemon juice
2 tablespoons olive oil
1 clove garlic, crushed
¼ teaspoon salt
Dash pepper

Cook artichoke hearts; drain. Mix remaining ingredients and pour over artichokes. Chill, spooning marinade over a few times. Drain; dash with paprika and serve.

Creamed Sweetbreads

1 pound sweetbreads, cooked*
    and partially cooled
6 tablespoons butter or margarine
3 tablespoons all-purpose flour
½ teaspoon salt and dash paprika
1 cup canned chicken broth
½ cup light cream
1 3-ounce can (⅔ cup) broiled
    sliced mushrooms, drained
2 tablespoons cooking sherry
1 package frozen patty shells, baked

Remove membrane from cooled sweet-breads. Melt butter, blend in flour, salt, paprika. Add broth, cream; cook and stir till thickened; add sweetbreads, mushrooms, and sherry. Heat. Serve in patty shells. Trim with parsley fluffs. Serves 6.

To cook sweetbreads: To 2 cups boiling water, add 1 tablespoon vinegar, 1 small bay leaf, and ½ teaspoon *each* pickling spices and salt. Add sweetbreads; simmer covered 20 minutes or till tender. Drain.

Oven-warm Baked Fruit Compote parades canned apricots, peaches, plums, under toasty coconut "snow." Oranges, lemon peel add zip.

- -

Be My Valentine

Chilled Tomato Juice
Chicken Livers in Red Wine
Sliced Avocado with Lemon
Baked Fruit Compote
Cheesecake Tassies   Coffee

- -

Chicken Livers in Red Wine

Cook 4 slices bacon till crisp; remove from skillet. Add 2 tablespoons *each* finely chopped onion and green pepper to the drippings; cook till tender but not brown.

Dredge 1 pound chicken livers in flour and add; cook 3 minutes.

Add ½ cup red wine (or use cream or milk, if desired), 1 tablespoon parsley flakes, dash thyme, ¼ teaspoon salt, and dash pepper. Cook 7 minutes. Stir in ½ cup pitted ripe olives, sliced.

Split, toast, and butter 8 small English muffins; serve chicken livers over. Crumble bacon atop. Makes 8 servings.

Baked Fruit Compote

1 1-pound can apricot halves, drained
1 1-pound can purple plums, drained
1 1-pound can peach halves, drained
3 or 4 thin slices orange, halved
½ cup orange juice
¼ cup brown sugar
½ teaspoon shredded lemon peel
2 tablespoons butter, melted
½ cup flaked coconut

In shallow baking dish, line up apricots and plums, alternate peach halves with orange slices. Mix juice, sugar, and peel; pour over. Drizzle butter over plums; sprinkle coconut over all. Bake at 425° for 15 minutes. Makes 8 servings.

Cheesecake Tassies

Crust: Soften ½ cup butter. Add *⅓ of an 8-ounce package* cream cheese and 1 tablespoon sugar; cream. Sift 1 cup sifted all-purpose flour with ¼ teaspoon cinnamon; add gradually to creamed mixture, blending well. Divide into 24 1-inch balls. Chill about 2 hours. Then press each ball into a 1¾-inch muffin (tassie) pan.

Filling: Cream together remaining two-thirds of the cream cheese and ¼ cup sugar. Add 1 egg and ¼ teaspoon vanilla; beat thoroughly. Pour into unbaked shells.

Bake at 350° for about 20 minutes. Loosen in pans. Cool slightly; remove carefully. Chill. Spread tops with dairy sour cream (takes ½ cup). Place one ripe strawberry on each, if desired. Makes 24.

Weekend-guest brunches

Company Eggs 'n Bacon

Creamed Eggs a la Asparagus
Toast   Spiced Crab Apples
Bacon   Canadian Bacon
Hot Coffee

Copenhagen Breakfast

Strawberries
Spiced Porridge
Hard-cooked Eggs
Cheese and Boiled-ham Platter
Danish Coffee Ring   Coffee

Creamed Eggs a la Asparagus

Cook one 10-ounce package frozen asparagus spears; drain. Melt 3 tablespoons butter; blend in 3 tablespoons flour. Add $1\frac{3}{4}$ cups milk; cook and stir till thick.

Season with salt and pepper. Add $\frac{1}{2}$ cup shredded sharp process cheese; stir till melted. Fold in 5 hard-cooked eggs, sliced. Arrange the hot asparagus spears on top. Sprinkle with paprika. Serve over hot toast. Makes 4 servings. See picture below.

Spiced Porridge

Scald 2 cups milk in double boiler. Stir in 1 tablespoon sugar, $\frac{1}{4}$ teaspoon *each* salt and ground cardamom, $\frac{1}{2}$ cup currants, and $\frac{1}{4}$ cup farina.

Cover; cook 30 minutes over hot, not boiling water; stir occasionally.

Spoon into 4 bowls. Top each serving with a pat of butter; sprinkle with brown sugar and cinnamon. Pass cream. Serves 4.

Company Eggs 'n Bacon Eggs go fancy in cheese sauce, with asparagus spears atop. Serve on buttery toast. Pass *two* kinds of bacon, perky crab apples, coffee. Keep hot with handy electric helpers!

Danish Coffee Ring

1 cake compressed yeast
¼ cup lukewarm water
½ cup milk, scalded
¼ cup shortening
¼ cup sugar
½ teaspoon salt
1 slightly beaten egg
½ teaspoon vanilla
1 teaspoon grated lemon peel
2½ to 3 cups sifted all-purpose flour
2 tablespoons butter, melted
½ cup raisins
½ cup slivered almonds, toasted
⅓ cup sugar
½ teaspoon mace *or*
   1½ teaspoons cinnamon

Soften yeast in lukewarm water. Combine next 4 ingredients; cool to lukewarm. Add the egg. Add vanilla, lemon peel, and *1 cup* of the flour; beat well. Stir in softened yeast; mix well. Add remaining flour to make a smooth, soft dough.

Knead on floured surface till smooth and elastic. Place in greased bowl, turning once to grease surface of dough. Cover and let rise till double, about 1½ hours.

Punch down. Let rest, covered, 10 minutes. Roll to 21x7 inches, ¼ inch thick.*

Brush with melted butter. Combine remaining ingredients; spread on dough. Roll from long edge; seal. Shape ring on greased cooky sheet. With scissors, snip almost to center at 1-inch intervals. Pull sections apart; twist slightly. Cover, let rise till double, about 50 minutes.

Bake at 375° for 20 minutes. Frost with Icing: Mix 1 cup sifted confectioners' sugar, 4 teaspoons milk, ½ teaspoon vanilla, and dash salt. Makes 1 large ring.

*To make 2 small rings, divide dough in half; roll each piece to 13x6 inches.

Petit Dejeuner

Breakfast Salad
Croissants
Butter Balls   Currant Jelly
Parisian Chocolate

Breakfast Salad

Arrange 3 chilled canned plums on each plate; radiate chilled fresh orange sections from them. Pass confectioners' sugar.

Croissants

1½ cups butter
⅓ cup sifted all-purpose flour
2 packages active dry yeast
¼ cup warm water
1 cup milk, scalded
¼ cup sugar
1 teaspoon salt
1 beaten egg
3¾ to 4 cups sifted
   all-purpose flour
1 egg yolk
1 tablespoon milk

Cream butter with ⅓ cup flour. Roll mixture between 2 sheets of waxed paper to form a 12x6-inch rectangle. Chill.

Soften yeast in warm water. Combine milk, sugar, and salt. Cool to lukewarm. Add softened yeast and egg. Mix well. Add 3¾ cups flour (or enough to make *soft* dough). Knead on lightly floured surface till smooth and glossy, about 5 minutes. On floured surface, roll dough in 14-inch square.

Place chilled butter on half the dough. Fold over other half of dough, sealing edges well. Roll to 20x12-inch rectangle.

Fold in thirds so you have 3 layers. (If butter softens, chill after each rolling.) Roll to 20x12-inches again. Fold and roll twice more. Then fold in thirds to form 12x7-inch rectangle. Chill 30 minutes.

Cut dough crosswise in fourths. Roll each fourth (keep remainder chilled) in 22x7-inch rectangle, ⅛ inch thick. Cut in 10 pie-shaped wedges, 4 inches at base and 7 inches long (you will have an extra ½-wedge on each end; put together, if desired).

To shape Croissants: Begin with base (if dough has shrunk back, pull to original size) and roll loosely toward point. Place 3 inches apart on ungreased baking sheet with center point down; curve ends to form crescents. Cover and let rise till almost double, about 1 hour.

Beat egg yolk with milk; brush on rolls. Bake at 375° for 12 to 15 minutes or till lightly browned. Serve warm. Makes 40. (Reheat in roll warmer or *very slow* oven.)

Parisian Chocolate

Combine 2½ one-ounce squares unsweetened chocolate and ½ cup water; stir over low heat till chocolate melts. Add ⅔ cup sugar and ½ teaspoon salt. Bring to boiling, reduce heat, and simmer 4 minutes. Cool to room temperature. Fold in ½ cup whipping cream, whipped. (You can keep this "batter" in refrigerator several days.)

To serve, place 1 heaping tablespoon chocolate in each teacup and fill with hot milk; stir well. Makes 8 to 10 servings.

Come and Get It

Strawberries and Pineapple Chunks
Easy Scrambled Eggs Grilled Ham
Dixie Coffee Bread   Hot Coffee

Easy Scrambled Eggs

Cut 1 inch off stick of butter; drop in skillet (not over heat). Break in 4 eggs. Pour in 3 to 4 tablespoons milk. Season.

Place over medium heat. With spoon, break up yolks and whites (don't beat); steer butter over skillet. Stir as mixture thickens; cook till just set. Serves 3.

Dixie Coffee Bread

Sift together 1½ cups sifted all-purpose flour, ¼ cup sugar, 4 teaspoons baking powder, and ½ teaspoon salt. Stir in ¾ cup corn meal. Add ¾ cup milk, 2 slightly beaten eggs, and ½ cup salad oil or cooled melted shortening. Pour into greased 9x9x 2-inch pan. Bake at 400° 15 minutes.

Blend ½ cup *each* brown sugar and peanut butter. Gradually add ⅓ cup milk, beating till fluffy. Spread over the baked corn bread; sprinkle with ½ cup coarsely chopped peanuts. Bake 5 minutes longer.

Favorites you can't beat   The aromas of sizzling ham (broiled or grilled — see index) and brewing coffee will call down the sleepiest guest. Add creamy eggs, oven-warm coffee bread, chilled fruit — umm!

Cherry-Cheese Tarts

    3 sticks pastry mix, *or* 1 recipe
        pastry calling for 3 cups flour
    2 cups milk
    1 2¼-ounce package custard-flavor
        dessert mix
    1 8-ounce package cream cheese, cubed
    ½ teaspoon vanilla
    1 No. 2 can cherry-pie filling

Roll pastry mix to ⅛-inch. Cut twelve 5-inch circles; fit over inverted muffin pans; pinch corners together; prick. Bake at 450° for 10 to 12 minutes. Cool.

Gradually add milk to dessert mix. Cook and stir over medium heat till mixture comes to *full* boil; cook 3 minutes. Remove from heat; add cream cheese and vanilla; beat smooth with rotary beater. Cool 10 minutes, stirring occasionally. Spoon into tart shells. Carefully spoon chilled cherry-pie filling atop. Chill firm. Makes 12.

To match picture: Cut 2½x¼-inch pastry strips. Bake beside tarts about 7 minutes. Top each tart with lattice of 4 baked pastry strips. Brush edges of tarts with corn syrup; sprinkle with chopped pistachio nuts (takes about ½ cup).

Cafe au Lait

    1 cup milk
    1 cup light cream
    3 tablespoons instant coffee
    2 cups boiling water

Heat milk and cream over low heat. Dissolve coffee in the boiling water. Beat milk mixture till foamy. Pour milk into one warmed server and coffee into another.

To serve: Fill cups from both pitchers at once, making streams meet en route.

Brioche

Start these double-deckers the night before—

1 package active dry yeast *or*
    1 cake compressed yeast
¼ cup water
½ cup milk, scalded and cooled
½ cup butter or margarine
⅓ cup sugar
½ teaspoon salt
3¼ cups sifted all-purpose flour
3 beaten eggs
1 beaten egg yolk
1 slightly beaten egg white
1 tablespoon sugar

Soften active dry yeast in *warm* water, compressed yeast in *lukewarm* water.

Meanwhile, cream butter; add ⅓ cup sugar and salt, creaming well. Add lukewarm milk; stir in *1 cup* of flour. Add yeast, eggs, and egg yolk; beat well. Stir in remaining flour; beat 5 to 8 minutes. Cover; let rise till a little more than double (about 2 hours); stir down; beat well. Cover *tightly* with foil; chill overnight.

Stir down; turn out on floured surface. Divide dough in fourths; set one section aside. Cut the other three sections in half; form each piece in 4 balls (24). Form reserved section in 24 smaller balls.

Place large balls in greased muffin pans. Poke indentation in top of each; moisten hole *slightly* with water; press small ball in each indentation. Cover; let rise in warm place till double (about 1 hour).

Combine egg white and 1 tablespoon sugar; brush tops. Bake at 375° about 15 minutes. Serve warm. Makes 24.

Butter Curls

Dip butter curler in hot water; pull lightly over a pound of firm butter, making curls about ⅛ inch thick. Repeat hot-water dip each time. Have butter firmer than from butter keeper, but not hard.

Go Parisian with fancy coffee—

Start with a classic continental breakfast (Cafe au Lait, airy rolls, butter curls); add fancy tarts, fruit, and cheese. Elegant!

Recipe roundup

Here are the surprises. For instance: Bananas in Nectar, or Wheat 'n Honey Butter, to cheer family at breakfast. Here are the specialties. For example: Flaky Danish Crescent, worthy of your fanciest brunch. Here is the "something different." Like: Swedish Eggs and Shrimp for lunch. These foods are fun to cook and fun to eat.

Brunch or lunch — the table's set

What a beautiful morning! Start it off with spicy Raisin-stuffed Apples, ready in a wink. Pass a platter of sunny-side eggs, crisp Fried Cornmeal Mush, sizzling Broiled Ham Slices. Go-with: hot Popovers.

Simple, cool, delicious — it's an easy Dutch lunch. Everyone helps himself to molded Tuna Ring, salami roll-ups and juicy tomatoes. For sandwiches, offer ham, Swiss cheese, crusty rye, and relishes.

Show-off salads for lunch

Corn in Tomato Cups   *Macaroni-Cheese Toss*   *Garlic Toast*

Fresh Fruit Medley

In large salad bowl, arrange small, pared watermelon wedges (chilled) as dividers (see picture below). Between dividers, place separate mounds of peach slices with banana cuts*, halved avocado rings*, orange sections, halved pineapple rings, cantaloupe and watermelon balls.

Center with flaked coconut. Trim with mint sprigs. Offer Marshmallow Dressing.

*To keep these fruits bright, use color keeper (ascorbic acid mixture) or dip in lemon juice mixed with a little water.

Tuna Ring   *Fresh Fruit Medley*   *Strawberry-Cream Squares*

Marshmallow Dressing

2 egg yolks
1 teaspoon sugar
¼ teaspoon dry mustard
1 tablespoon vinegar
½ cup tiny marshmallows
½ cup whipping cream, whipped

Beat egg yolks; add next 4 ingredients. Cook and stir over low heat till marshmallows melt and mixture thickens. Cool thoroughly. Stir till smooth, then fold in whipped cream. Makes about 1 cup.

Corn in Tomato Cups

8 large ripe tomatoes
1 12-ounce can (1½ cups) Mexican-style whole kernel corn, drained
1 large cucumber, diced
1 teaspoon grated onion
4 slices bacon, crisp-cooked and coarsely crumbled
¼ cup clear French dressing
½ teaspoon salt
Dash pepper

Peel tomatoes, if desired. With sharp knife cut cone shape from end opposite stem of each tomato; reserve. Hollow out center. If wobbly, cut off thin slices at stem end. Turn upside down to drain; chill.

Combine remaining ingredients; chill. Sprinkle inside of tomatoes with salt. Spoon salad into tomato shells; arrange on lettuce. Perch a cone, point up, on each. Offer mayonnaise. Makes 8 servings.

Potato-salad Mold

This fancy salad's delicious with cold cuts and cheese — makes a dandy company lunch!

1 envelope (1 tablespoon) unflavored gelatin
2 tablespoons sugar
1 teaspoon salt
1¼ cups boiling water
¼ cup lemon juice

• • •

8 stuffed green olives, sliced
3 hard-cooked eggs, chopped
4 cups diced cooked potatoes
1 cup diced celery
¼ cup diced green pepper
¼ cup diced pimiento
¼ cup chopped green onions
¼ cup chopped parsley
1½ teaspoons salt
1 cup mayonnaise

• • •

½ cup whipping cream, whipped

Mix gelatin, sugar, and salt thoroughly; pour boiling water over and stir well to dissolve sugar. Add lemon juice. Pour a thin layer of the mixture into a 1½-quart ring mold; chill till almost firm. Arrange olive slices and green-pepper strips on gelatin to form "flower" design.

Add olives, eggs, vegetables, salt, and mayonnaise to remaining gelatin mixture. Fold in whipped cream. Spoon over gelatin layer in mold. Chill until firm. Serves 8.

Serve with tomato cuts, Swiss cheese, ham, and salami roll-ups, and rye bread.

Chef's trick for coring lettuce: Remove droopy leaves. Smack the head stem end down on counter top. Then, twist core right out!

Fix romaine French-style for tossed salad: Cut rib out of each leaf in two strokes. To trim bowl, snip leaves in points with scissors.

Tuna Ring

1 envelope (1 tablespoon) unflavored
   gelatin
¼ cup cold water
* * *
1 can condensed tomato soup
1 3-ounce package cream cheese
1 cup salad dressing or mayonnaise
½ cup chopped celery
½ cup sliced stuffed green olives
¼ cup chopped green pepper
¼ cup sliced green onions
¼ cup chopped pimiento
2 hard-cooked eggs, chopped
2 6½- or 7-ounce cans (2 cups)
   tuna, in chunks

Soften gelatin in cold water. Heat soup to
boiling. Add gelatin; stir till dissolved. Add
cream cheese, beat smooth with electric or
rotary beater. Blend in salad dressing; stir
in remaining ingredients.

Pour into a 5-cup ring mold; chill firm.
To serve, garnish with greens (see picture
page 45). Makes 6 to 8 servings.

Macaroni-Cheese Toss

*A man's kind of salad — chock full of Cheddar
and tossed with tangy dressing—*

½ pound (2 cups) small shell macaroni
3 tablespoons clear French dressing
* * *
¼ pound sharp Cheddar cheese,
   cubed (1 cup)
3 hard-cooked eggs, cubed
1 cup drained cooked or canned peas
½ cup chopped celery
½ cup sliced green onions
⅓ cup mayonnaise or salad dressing
1 tablespoon prepared mustard
1½ teaspoons prepared horseradish
½ teaspoon Worcestershire sauce
Dash salt
Dash seasoned salt
Dash pepper

Cook macaroni in boiling salted water till
tender; drain and cool. Pour French dressing over macaroni and set aside. Combine
cheese, eggs, and vegetables. Blend mayonnaise and seasonings; pour over cheese
mixture. Add macaroni; toss to mix. Chill.

Serve in bowl lined with greens; top with
cherry tomatoes. Makes 8 to 10 servings.

Guacamole Salad Bowl

½ medium head lettuce
2 tomatoes, cut in wedges
½ cup sliced pitted ripe olives
¼ cup chopped green onions
1 cup corn chips
1 6½-, 7-, or 9¼-ounce can
   tuna, drained
1 recipe Avocado Dressing
½ cup shredded Cheddar cheese

Break lettuce into bowl. Add next five ingredients. Toss lightly with Avocado Dressing. Top with cheese and additional ripe
olives. Makes 4 servings.

Avocado Dressing

½ cup mashed ripe avocado
1 tablespoon lemon juice
½ cup dairy sour cream
⅓ cup salad oil
1 clove garlic, crushed
½ teaspoon sugar
½ teaspoon chili powder
¼ teaspoon salt
¼ teaspoon bottled hot pepper sauce

Combine ingredients; beat with electric
beater or blender. Use the same day.
Makes about 1½ cups dressing.

Strawberry-Cream Squares

2 3-ounce packages strawberry-
   flavored gelatin
2 cups boiling water
2 10-ounce packages frozen
   strawberries
1 13½-ounce can (1½ cups)
   crushed pineapple
2 large, fully ripe bananas,
   finely diced
* * *
1 cup dairy sour cream

Dissolve gelatin in boiling water. Add berries, stirring occasionally till thawed. Add
pineapple and banana. Pour *half* the mixture into an 8x8x2-inch pan. Chill till firm.
Spoon sour cream over chilled gelatin,
spreading in an even layer; pour remaining
gelatin over. Chill firm.

Cut in 9 squares; serve on lettuce ruffles.
Garnish with dollops of sour cream and
whole strawberries split in half from top
almost to bottom. Makes 9 servings.

Fruit fix-ups

California Fruit Bowl

1 1-pound box (3 cups) dried prunes
1 3-inch stick cinnamon, broken up
1 unpared medium orange, cut in
    ¼-inch slices
⅓ cup brown sugar

Rinse prunes, then just cover with water.
Add cinnamon. Cover; bring to boil, then
simmer for 20 minutes. Add the orange
slices and sugar. Cover and cook 5 minutes
longer. Cool. Makes 6 servings.

Rhubarb Sauce on Bananas

Combine 3 cups rhubarb cut in 1-inch
pieces, ½ to ¾ cup sugar, and ¼ cup water. Bring to boiling; cover; cook slowly 5
minutes. Chill. Serve over banana slices.

Bananas in Nectar

Fill 4 chilled sherbet dishes with sliced
bananas. Add enough frosty-cold guava,
papaya, or apricot nectar to cover.

Garnish fruit with mandarin-orange
sections, maraschino cherries, and sprigs
of mint. Makes 4 servings.

Raisin-stuffed Apples

4 large baking apples
¼ cup brown sugar
½ cup seedless raisins
Butter
½ cup water

Core apples; pare strip from center or top
of each. Mix brown sugar and raisins.
Place about 2 tablespoons of raisin mixture
in center of each apple; dot with butter.*
Place apples in large saucepan; add water. Cover tightly; bring to boil. Continue
boiling gently 15 minutes, or till tender.
Serve warm. Makes 4 servings.

*Omit butter if serving apples chilled.

Broiled Grapefruit
*(from Chalet Suzanne,
Lake Wales, Florida)*

2 large grapefruits, halved
¼ to ⅓ cup butter
2 teaspoons sugar
½ cup cinnamon-sugar mixture
    (1 part cinnamon to 4 parts sugar)

Have fruit at room temperature so it will
be hot through when top is browned. Cut
around every section of each half, close to
membrane so fruit is completely loosened
from shell. Cut hole in center of each half;
fill with 1 to 1½ tablespoons butter. Sprinkle each with ½ teaspoon sugar, then with
2 tablespoons cinnamon mixture.

Broil 4 inches from heat 8 to 10 minutes,
or till tops are brown. Serves 4.

*Breakfast Berry Bowl —
a snappy fruit trio
to brighten the morn*

Chill 1 No. 2 can (2½ cups) pineapple chunks; drain, reserving syrup. Rinse 1 pint *each* of fresh red
raspberries and strawberries; slice
the strawberries. In crystal bowl
(if you have one), arrange the
strawberries, then the pineapple
chunks; top with the raspberries.
Pour chilled pineapple syrup over.
Serve with cream. Serves 6.

Lunch-and-brunch meats

Breakfast Hash

2 tablespoons butter or margarine
About ½ pound leftover cooked beef,
  ground (2 cups)
2 cups *finely diced* raw potato
⅓ cup finely chopped onion
½ cup beef broth
½ teaspoon salt
• • •
4 eggs

Melt butter in skillet; add beef, potato, onion, broth and salt; mix well. Cover and cook over low heat, stirring often, till potatoes are tender, about 15 minutes.

During last 3 to 5 minutes hash is cooking, slip the eggs into boiling water or egg poacher; cook to desired doneness.

Serve hash on 4 plates, making slight indentation in center. Place a poached egg atop each serving. Makes 4 servings.

Broiled Ham Slice

Broiled: Select 1-inch ham (or picnic) slice; trim rind, if any. Slash fat edge in several places. Broil 3 inches from heat; turn once. Broil *fully cooked* slice 15 minutes total; an *uncooked* slice (cook-before-eating type) for 18 to 20 minutes total.

Pan-broiled: Choose ¼- to ½-inch thick slice of smoked ham (or picnic). Rub heavy skillet with ham fat. Over low heat, pan-broil ½-inch slice of *fully cooked* ham 3 to 4 minutes each side; a ½-inch slice *uncooked* ham for 6 to 8 minutes on each side.

Pan-fried Sausage

Patties: Buy or shape bulk pork sausage in a roll; cut in thin patties. Pan-fry slowly, starting in a cold skillet. Turn once. Cook 15 to 20 minutes.

Links: Place in cold skillet; add ¼ cup cold water. Cover and cook slowly 5 minutes; drain. Uncover and fry slowly, turning with tongs till all sides are brown. Do not prick. Takes 12 to 14 minutes.

Canadian-style Bacon

Broiled: Broil ¼-inch slices 3 inches from heat, 1 to 2 minutes on each side.

Pan-broiled: Preheat skillet; brush with oil. Brown ¼-inch slices quickly, about 2 to 3 minutes on each side.

Breakfast Steaks

Select 2½- to 3½-ounce steaks, from beef round, sirloin tip, or shoulder. Use meat tenderizer following label directions. In hot lightly greased skillet, pan-broil about 2 minutes per side—use high heat. Don't overcook! Serve with butter-browned peach halves.

Creamed Dried Beef

¼ pound dried beef, shredded
2 tablespoons butter or margarine
2 tablespoons all-purpose flour
1¼ cups milk
½ teaspoon Worcestershire sauce
Toast points or chow-mein noodles

Cook dried beef in butter till edges frizzle. Blend flour and milk. Add to beef. Cook and stir till thick. Add Worcestershire. Season with pepper. Spoon over toast or crisp noodles. Makes 4 servings.

Trout Amandine

4 small fresh-water trout, cleaned
Seasoned flour
½ cup butter
2 tablespoons slivered almonds
¼ cup lemon juice
2 tablespoons snipped parsley

Wash fish; dry thoroughly. Dip in flour. Brown in ¼ *cup* of the butter, 12 to 15 minutes, turning once. Remove to platter; keep warm. Melt remaining butter in the skillet. Add almonds; brown, stirring occasionally. Stir in lemon juice and parsley; season to taste. Pour over warm trout and serve. Makes 4 luncheon servings.

So-delicious cereals

Hominy Fluff with Hash

1 cup quick-cooking hominy grits
2½ cups milk
2½ cups water
1¼ teaspoons salt
2 tablespoons butter or margarine
¼ cup snipped parsley
3 slightly beaten egg yolks
3 egg whites

• • •

1 1-pound can corned-beef hash,
   heated

Cook hominy grits, milk, water, salt, and butter about 5 minutes or till thick, stirring frequently. Cool 10 minutes and stir in parsley and egg yolks.

Add dash salt to egg whites, beat till stiff; fold into grits mixture. Pour into buttered 6½-cup ring mold. Place in shallow pan; pour in hot water to depth of 1 inch. Bake at 325° for 1¼ hours or till knife inserted comes out clean. Unmold; fill center with hot corned-beef hash. Serves 6 to 8.

Bacon Spoon Bread

¾ cup corn meal
1½ cups cold water
2 cups shredded, sharp Cheddar cheese
¼ cup soft butter or margarine
2 cloves garlic, crushed
½ teaspoon salt
1 cup milk
5 well-beaten egg yolks
½ pound sliced bacon, crisp-cooked,
   drained, and crumbled
4 stiff-beaten egg whites

Combine corn meal and water; cook and stir till consistency of mush. Remove from heat. Add next 4 ingredients; stir to melt cheese. Gradually add milk. Stir in egg yolks; add bacon (reserving some for garnish, if desired). Fold in egg whites.

Pour mixture into greased 2-quart souffle dish or casserole. Bake at 325° for 65 minutes or till done. Spoon into warm dishes; top with butter. Makes 6 servings.

Gnocchi

3 cups milk
¼ cup butter or margarine
1 teaspoon salt
¾ cup farina
2 slightly beaten eggs
1 cup shredded Parmesan cheese
¼ cup butter or margarine

Combine first 3 ingredients. Scald (do not boil). Stirring constantly, add farina in fine stream. Cook and stir till thick.

Beat in eggs and *half* of cheese. Pour into greased 8x8x2-inch pan. Chill firm. Cut in slices ½-inch thick (4 inches long). Overlap in greased 13x9x2-inch pan. Dot with butter; sprinkle with remaining cheese. Bake at 425° for 25 to 30 minutes. Serves 6.

Wheat 'n Honey Butter

Add 1 teaspoon salt to 5 cups rapidly boiling water. Gradually sprinkle in 1 cup toasted wheat cereal (water shouldn't stop boiling). Cook about 15 minutes. Serve with Honey Butter. Makes 4 servings.

Honey Butter: Whip ½ cup butter till fluffy. Gradually add ½ cup honey; beat.

Scrapple

1½ pounds bulk pork sausage
1 teaspoon salt
½ teaspoon sage
1 cup yellow corn meal

In saucepan, break sausage in small pieces. Add 4 cups water, stirring to separate meat. Heat to boiling; reduce heat; simmer 20 minutes. Drain meat; reserving 3 cups of stock. Add salt and sage to stock; bring to boiling. Combine corn meal and 1 cup cold water; gradually stir into stock.

Cover; cook over low heat 10 minutes, stirring occasionally. Add sausage, pour into 9½x5x3-inch loaf pan. Cool; chill overnight. Slice, fry and serve as for Fried Corn-meal Mush. Makes 9 servings.

Fried Corn-meal Mush

2¾ cups water
1 cup corn meal
1 cup cold water
1 teaspoon salt
1 teaspoon sugar (optional)

In saucepan, heat 2¾ cups water to boiling. Combine remaining ingredients; gradually add to boiling water, stirring constantly. Cook till mixture thickens, stirring frequently. Cover, continue cooking over *low* heat 10 to 15 minutes.

Pour into a 7½x3½x2¼-inch loaf pan. Cool. Chill overnight. Slice ½-inch thick. Fry in small amount hot fat till brown, turning once. Makes 6 servings.

It's sizzling good—fried mush!

Fill a platter with crunchy Fried Corn-meal Mush and crisp bacon for a wonderful breakfast or supper. Delicious with butter, warm maple-flavored syrup, honey, or jelly.

1 To cook mush: In small bowl, mix the corn meal with *cold* water (this prevents lumps). Then, add salt, and a little sugar. Gradually stir mixture into *boiling* water.

2 Pour mush into small loaf pan to mold. Cool, then chill thoroughly. Or, style dainty, round slices: Mold in small frozen-juice-concentrate cans. Nice for brunches.

3 To unmold, just run a spatula or knife around edge of mush to loosen. Turn out on board; cut in slices. Fry plain, or dip in corn meal first, for extra-crunchy coat.

4 Fry in hot fat on griddle or in skillet. (Drop of water will dance when griddle is hot enough.) Fry slowly, adding more fat if needed. Takes about 7 minutes on a side.

Eggs in exciting ways

Eggs Goldenrod

6 hard-cooked eggs
3 tablespoons butter or margarine
3 tablespoons all-purpose flour
½ teaspoon salt
1½ cups milk
6 slices hot toast, quartered

Chop egg whites and sieve yolks. Melt butter; blend in flour and salt. Add milk all at once. Cook and stir till mixture thickens and bubbles. Add the chopped egg whites; heat briefly. Ladle creamed mixture over toast. Sprinkle sieved yolks atop. Pass salt and pepper. Makes 6 servings.

Baked Eggs with Cheese

4 eggs
¼ cup light cream
½ cup shredded sharp process cheese

Butter 4 ramekins or custard cups. In each put 1 tablespoon cream. Break one egg into each; sprinkle with salt and pepper. Set cups in shallow pan and pour hot water in pan to depth of 1 inch.

Bake in slow oven (325°) 15 minutes. Top each egg with about 2 tablespoons of the cheese; bake 5 to 10 minutes longer. Serve at once. Makes 4 servings.

Eggs Goldenrod

A delicious old favorite—hard-cooked egg whites are chunked into creamy white sauce, spooned over hot toast. Atop go sieved yolks!

French Omelet

2 eggs
Dash salt
Dash pepper
1 teaspoon butter, or olive oil

• • •

¼ cup grated Cheddar cheese, or
pan-fried onions or mushrooms

With a fork beat eggs, salt, and pepper together till blended but not frothy. Heat an
8-inch omelet pan. Add butter and melt,
tilting pan to grease sides. When butter
has browned lightly, or oil forms ripples,
pour in omelet mixture, leaving heat mod-
erately high. With fork tines up and parallel
to skillet, rapidly stir through top of uncooked egg. Keep omelet an even depth.
Stir the uncooked egg zigzag fashion, out
to the edges. Shake pan all the while to
keep egg mixture moving.

When egg is mostly set and bottom is
just beginning to brown lightly, remove pan
from heat. (Omelet cooks in about 1 minute.) Spoon cheese, onions or mushrooms
across center, at right angles to handle of
pan. Flip top third of omelet (near handle)
over filling. Grasp handle with the palm up
and tilt skillet, handle up, over a hot plate
so the partly folded omelet slides to the far
side of pan. Slide ⅓ of the omelet onto the
plate then tilt the pan over, thus folding the
omelet neatly in thirds. Makes 1 serving.

Creamed Eggs Elegante

4 rusks, buttered
2 tablespoons prepared mustard
1 4½-ounce can deviled ham

• • •

4 hard-cooked eggs
1 can condensed cream of
mushroom soup
¼ cup milk
2 tablespoons finely chopped onion
Dash Worcestershire sauce

Spread rusks with mustard, then with ham.
Place in slow oven (325°) 10 minutes, or
till warm through. Meanwhile, chop 2 of
the eggs; combine with remaining ingredients; heat. To serve, place each rusk on
a plate; spoon sauce over. Slice remaining
eggs; arrange slices on rusks. Sprinkle with
paprika; trim with parsley. Serves 4.

Stir rapidly in zigzag fashion

Shake—keep omelet moving

Tilt, handle up; roll omelet out

Rainbow Eggs

Tint peeled eggs in a variety of colors; serve as the good-to-eat trim on a luncheon platter—

Place eggs in saucepan and cover with cold water (at least 1 inch above eggs). Bring to boiling; turn off heat (if more than 4 eggs, reduce heat to keep water just below *simmering*). Cover and leave eggs in water 15 to 20 minutes.

Cool eggs promptly in cold water to stop cooking, help prevent dark surface on yolk.

For each color, dissolve an envelope of fruit-flavored soft-drink powder in 1 cup water (*or* tint water with food coloring)— mix enough of each to cover eggs.

Shell eggs; place in tinted water. Let stand till of desired shade.

Dry the tinted eggs on paper towels. Arrange on "nests" of shredded carrot or on fluffy lettuce for colorful trim.

Hollandaise Sauce

A tangy golden sauce that adds the final touch to Eggs Benedict. Just dandy served over broccoli, asparagus, or cauliflower, too!

    4 egg yolks
    1 to 2 tablespoons lemon juice
        • • •
    ½ pound (2 sticks or 1 cup)
        butter, melted
    ¼ teaspoon salt
    Dash pepper

In top of a double boiler, beat egg yolks slightly and stir in lemon juice. Place over *hot, but not boiling water* — don't allow water in bottom pan to touch top pan.

Add the butter a little at a time, stirring constantly with wooden spoon. Add the salt and pepper to taste. Continue cooking slowly just until mixture thickens – stir constantly. Makes 1 cup.

A touch of glamour – Eggs Benedict from Brennan's in New Orleans.

Eggs Benedict

A "traditional Brennan breakfast" is Eggs Benedict followed by hearty sirloin, hot French bread, crepes Suzette and cafe au lait—

Top crisp rusks (or English muffins) with slices of grilled Canadian-style bacon and Soft-poached Eggs. Generously ladle Hollandaise Sauce over the eggs and sprinkle with paprika. To match picture, garnish with truffle slices and sprigs of parsley. Serve immediately.

Soft-poached Eggs

In large saucepan, heat water (3 or 4 inches deep) just to boiling. Add a little vinegar and salt. Break each egg into a sauce dish. Stir the simmering water to make a swirl and slip egg from dish right into middle of the swirl. Be sure to follow the swirl with the dish so egg goes into water in the same direction.

Turn heat down—don't let water boil. It takes 3 to 5 minutes for eggs to cook, depending on desired doneness. Remove eggs with a slotted spoon or pancake turner.

To keep hot till serving time, transfer eggs to warm water (about 3 inches deep).

Stuffed-egg Casserole

    3 tablespoons butter
    3 tablespoons all-purpose flour
    1 No. 2½ can (3½ cups) tomatoes
    ½ cup chopped onion
    2 teaspoons sugar
    ¾ teaspoon salt
    Dash pepper
          • • •
    6 hard-cooked eggs, deviled*
    ¾ cup fine dry bread crumbs
    2 tablespoons butter, melted

Melt butter; blend in flour. Add tomatoes, onion, sugar, salt, and pepper; cook till mixture thickens, stirring constantly. Pour into 10x6x1½-inch baking dish.

Arrange deviled eggs in the sauce. Combine crumbs and butter; sprinkle over eggs. Bake in a hot oven (425°) for 10 minutes or till hot. Serve over hot toast. Serves 6.

*Use your favorite recipe for deviled eggs, or see index listing for our recipe.

Swedish Eggs and Shrimp

It's a quick lunch, with pickled beets and rye bread. Dessert is vanilla ice cream with a sprinkle of peanuts—

    6 hard-cooked eggs, chilled
    2 to 3 cups cooked cleaned
      shrimp, chilled
    ½ cup whipping cream
    ½ cup mayonnaise
    ½ teaspoon shredded lemon peel
    ½ teaspoon dried dill weed or
      2 teaspoons finely snipped dill

Cut eggs in half lengthwise; arrange in center of serving dish. Circle eggs with generous rim of chilled shrimp.

Whip the cream to soft peaks. Combine the mayonnaise and lemon peel; fold in whipped cream. Spoon mixture over eggs; sprinkle with dill. Makes 4 servings.

Italian Rice Souffle

Team with green grape clusters and crisp apple salad for a delicious light lunch—

    ¾ cup uncooked rice
    2 cups milk
    6 tablespoons butter or margarine
    3 tablespoons all-purpose flour
    2 cups milk
    1½ teaspoons salt
    8 ounces Swiss cheese, shredded
      (about 2 cups)
    4 egg yolks
    4 egg whites

Cook rice uncovered in 2 cups milk over low heat till tender (about 15 minutes), stirring frequently with a fork. When all milk is absorbed, remove from heat.

Melt butter; stir in flour; cook and stir 1 minute. Remove from heat; gradually add 2 cups milk. Cook and stir till smooth, bubbly. Remove from heat. Add salt, cheese; stir till cheese melts. Add rice.

Beat egg yolks till thick and lemon-colored. Fold in cheese mixture; cool slightly. Beat egg whites to stiff peaks; fold cheese mixture into whites. Pour into *ungreased* 1½-quart souffle dish or casserole. Bake in moderate oven (350°) 65 minutes or till knife inserted comes out clean. Serve immediately. Makes 6 servings.

Breakfast breads

Orange-blossom Muffins

Crunchy-good outside; delicate flavor inside—

1 slightly beaten egg
½ cup orange juice
½ cup orange marmalade
2 cups packaged biscuit mix
½ cup chopped pecans

· · ·

¼ cup sugar
1 tablespoon all-purpose flour
½ teaspoon cinnamon
¼ teaspoon nutmeg
1 tablespoon butter or margarine

Combine slightly beaten egg, orange juice, and orange marmalade. Add biscuit mix and beat vigorously for 30 seconds. Stir in the chopped nuts. Line muffin pans with paper bake cups; fill about ½ full.

Combine sugar, flour, cinnamon, and nutmeg. Cut in butter till crumbly. Sprinkle over batter in paper bake cups.

Bake in hot oven (400°) for about 20 minutes or till done. Makes 16 muffins.

Graham Gems

Try these with butter and grape jelly—

½ cup sifted all-purpose flour
¼ cup sugar
1 teaspoon salt
4 teaspoons baking powder
1 cup stirred whole-wheat flour

· · ·

1 well-beaten egg
1 cup milk
3 tablespoons butter or
  margarine, melted

Sift together the flour, sugar, salt, and baking powder; stir in whole-wheat flour. Combine egg, milk, and butter.

Make a well in dry ingredients and add liquid all at once. Stir just till moistened. Fill greased muffin pans ⅔ full. Bake in hot oven (425°) 15 to 18 minutes or till done. Makes about 10 muffins.

William Tell Coffeecake

¼ cup butter or margarine
¾ cup sugar
1 egg
1 teaspoon vanilla
1½ cups sifted all-purpose flour
2 teaspoons baking powder
½ teaspoon nutmeg
¼ teaspoon salt
⅔ cup milk

· · ·

1 cup finely chopped pared
  tart apple
⅓ cup sugar
1 teaspoon cinnamon

Stir butter to soften; add sugar and cream till fluffy. Add egg and vanilla; beat well. Sift together dry ingredients; add to creamed mixture alternately with milk, beating smooth after each addition. Pour into greased 9x9x2-inch pan.

Combine remaining ingredients, sprinkle over batter. Bake in moderate oven (375°) 25 to 30 minutes or till done. Cool 15 minutes; cut in squares and serve warm.

Muffin-mix Coffeecake

½ package (1 packet) orange-
  muffin mix
2 tablespoons pineapple-
  apricot preserves

· · ·

3 tablespoons sugar
3 tablespoons all-purpose flour
2 tablespoons butter or margarine
3 tablespoons chopped
  California walnuts

Prepare batter from muffin mix according to package directions. Pour into greased 8x1½-inch round pan. Dot preserves (cut any large pieces) evenly over batter.

Sprinkle with *Streusel Topping:* Combine sugar and flour. Cut in butter till crumbly; stir in the chopped walnuts.

Bake in hot oven (400°) 18 to 20 minutes or till done. Cut into wedges. Serve warm.

Banana Ambrosia Ring

½ cup flaked coconut
⅓ cup maple-flavored syrup
2 tablespoons butter or
  margarine, melted

· · ·

2 cups packaged biscuit mix
3 tablespoons sugar
½ cup mashed ripe banana
1 slightly beaten egg
3 tablespoons butter or
  margarine, melted

· · ·

2 tablespoons sugar
1 teaspoon cinnamon
2 tablespoons butter or margarine

Mix coconut with the syrup and 2 tablespoons melted butter and spread over the bottom of a 6½-cup ring mold.

Combine biscuit mix and 3 tablespoons sugar. Stir in banana, egg, and 3 tablespoons melted butter. Beat mixture vigorously 1 minute. Spoon *half* the batter over coconut in mold.

Mix 2 tablespoons sugar with the cinnamon and butter; sprinkle over batter. Cover with remaining batter. Bake in moderate oven (375°) 20 minutes or till done. Invert to unmold. Serve warm.

Cinnamon Fantan Buns

1 package active dry yeast
½ cup milk, scalded
¼ cup sugar
¼ cup shortening
1 teaspoon salt
3 cups sifted all-purpose flour
1 egg
2 tablespoons butter, melted

Soften yeast in ¼ cup *warm* water. Combine next 4 ingredients; cool to lukewarm. Add *1 cup* of the flour; mix well. Stir in yeast, egg; beat well. Stir in 2 cups flour (or enough for soft dough).

Cover; let rest 10 minutes. Knead till satiny (8 minutes). Place in greased bowl; turn once to grease surface. Cover; let rise till double (1½ hours). Turn out; form in ball. Cover; let rest 10 minutes. Roll to 20x10 inches. Brush with butter.

Filling: Combine ⅓ cup chopped walnuts, ½ cup sugar, 1½ teaspoons cinnamon; sprinkle over dough.

Roll up from long side. Cut in eight 2½-inch lengths. *Without cutting through*, snip each length in thirds crosswise. Place on greased baking sheet; spread thirds to form fan. Cover; let almost double (25 minutes). Bake at 350° for 12 to 15 minutes.

Bring out this luscious Banana Ambrosia Ring at your fanciest brunch. The maple-flavored, chewy coconut topping makes it party-special.

Delight any sweet tooth with these Cinnamon Fantan Buns, brimful of crunchy nut filling. Fan-swirled shape makes each a 3-in-1 treat.

Flaky Danish Crescent

1 package active dry yeast
2 cups sifted all-purpose flour
1 tablespoon sugar
½ teaspoon salt
½ cup chilled butter or margarine
¼ cup milk, scalded and cooled
1 slightly beaten egg yolk
Filling
½ cup chopped almonds or pecans

Soften yeast in ¼ cup *warm* water. Sift together dry ingredients; cut in butter till some of mixture is like corn meal and some the size of peas. Mix cooled milk and egg yolk; add with softened yeast to flour mixture, stirring to make soft dough. Cover; chill a few hours or overnight.

Halve dough (keep half chilled). On floured surface roll one half to 12x9-inch rectangle, ⅛ inch thick. Reserve 2 tablespoons of Filling for the glaze; spread rolled dough with *half* of the *remainder*. Sprinkle with *half* the nuts.

Roll as for jellyroll from long side; seal edges and ends. Place seam down on cooky sheet. Shape in crescent; flatten slightly. Repeat with remaining dough.

Cover; let rise in warm place till almost double (about 1 hour). Brush with reserved Filling. To garnish, sprinkle with additional almonds, thinly sliced. Bake in moderate oven (375°) 20 minutes or till done. Serve warm. Makes 2 Crescents.

Filling: Combine ½ cup sugar and 1 teaspoon cinnamon, and fold into 1 stiff-beaten egg white.

Quickie Stickies

⅓ cup honey
3 tablespoons butter or
    margarine, melted
¼ cup broken California walnuts
1 package refrigerated biscuits
Melted butter or margarine
Cinnamon

Blend honey and butter; divide among 7 muffin cups. Sprinkle walnuts into each. Brush one side of each biscuit with butter; sprinkle with cinnamon. Cut in half. Place 3 halves, cut side down (curved side up) and buttered sides touching, in each muffin cup. (One will have only 2 halves.) Bake at 350° for 15 minutes. Makes 7.

Butter-Pecan Rolls

1 cake compressed yeast
¼ cup *lukewarm* water
1 cup milk, scalded
¼ cup shortening
¼ cup sugar
1 teaspoon salt
3¼ to 3½ cups sifted all-purpose flour
1 beaten egg
Filling and Topping

Soften yeast in lukewarm water. Combine next 4 ingredients; cool to lukewarm. Add *1 cup* of the flour; beat well. Beat in yeast and egg. Gradually add remaining flour to form a soft dough; beat well. Brush top *lightly* with soft shortening; cover and let rise in warm place till double (1½ to 2 hours). Punch down; turn out on lightly floured surface and divide dough in half. Roll each piece in 12x8-inch rectangle.

Filling: Brush each rectangle with 2 tablespoons melted butter. Combine ½ cup sugar and 2 teaspoons cinnamon; sprinkle half over each rectangle.

Roll each rectangle as for a jellyroll, beginning with long side; seal edge. Cut each roll in eight 1½-inch slices.

Topping: In *each* of two 9½x5x3-inch metal loaf pans, mix ½ cup brown sugar, ¼ cup butter and 1 tablespoon light corn syrup. Heat slowly, stirring frequently till blended. Remove from heat. Sprinkle ⅓ cup pecans in each pan.

Place 8 rolls cut side down, in each pan. Cover; let rise in warm place till double (35 to 45 minutes). Bake in moderate oven (375°) for 25 minutes or till done. Cool 2 or 3 minutes; invert on rack and remove pans. Makes 16 rolls.

Speedy Orange Coffeecake

1 package refrigerated biscuits
2 tablespoons butter, melted
¼ cup sugar
2 tablespoons finely chopped walnuts
2 teaspoons grated orange peel

Dip biscuits in butter, then in mixture of sugar, nuts, and peel. Overlap biscuits in circle in 9-inch pie plate.* Bake at 400° for 15 minutes or till done. Serve hot.

*Or make a double recipe and bake coffeecake in an 11-inch pie plate.

Walnut Coffeecake Sticks

¾ cup butter or
  margarine, softened
¾ cup brown sugar
1 tablespoon milk or light cream
1 teaspoon cinnamon
  • • •
1 unsliced sandwich loaf, about 11
  inches long
1 to 1½ cups chopped
  California walnuts

Cream together butter, sugar, milk, and cinnamon till light and fluffy.

Trim crusts from bread. Cut loaf crosswise in 3 equal, large cubes. Cut each cube in thirds, then in thirds again in opposite direction, making 9 sticks per cube. Spread butter mixture on all surfaces except bottom. Roll in nuts.

Bake on cooky sheet in moderate oven (375°) 15 minutes or till crispy Makes 27.

Popovers

2 eggs
1 cup milk
1 cup sifted all-purpose flour
½ teaspoon salt
1 tablespoon salad oil

Place eggs in bowl; add milk, flour, and salt. Beat 1½ minutes with rotary or electric beater. Add salad oil; beat ½ minute. (Don't overbeat.) Fill 6 to 8 *well-greased* custard cups ½ full.

Bake in very hot oven (475°) 15 minutes; reduce heat to 350° and bake 25 to 30 minutes or till browned and firm.

A few minutes before removing from oven, prick each popover with a fork to let steam escape. If you like them dry inside, turn off oven; leave them in 30 minutes, door ajar. Serve hot with butter, or split and serve with saucy filling. Makes 6 to 8.

Rich Butter-Pecan Rolls

Simply scrumptious! Under a coating of brown sugar and butter syrup, they're spicy with cinnamon and crunchy with nuts. Great served oven-hot with lots of butter.

Pancakes and waffles

Corn-meal Pancakes

1½ cups yellow cornmeal
¼ cup all-purpose flour
1 teaspoon *each* soda, salt, and sugar
2 cups buttermilk
2 tablespoons salad oil
1 slightly beaten egg yolk
1 stiff-beaten egg white

Stir together dry ingredients. Add buttermilk, oil, egg yolk; blend well. Fold in egg white. Let stand 10 minutes. Bake on hot, lightly greased griddle. Makes 16.

Blintz Pancakes

1 cup sifted all-purpose flour
1 tablespoon sugar
½ teaspoon salt
1 cup dairy sour cream
1 cup small-curd cottage cheese
4 well-beaten eggs

Sift dry ingredients into bowl. Add remaining ingredients; fold just till moistened. Bake on hot, lightly greased griddle. Serve with Blueberry Sauce. Makes 16 cakes.

Blueberry Sauce: Mix one 1-pound can blueberries, 2 teaspoons cornstarch; cook, stirring constantly till thickened. Add 1 teaspoon lemon juice.

Best-seller Buttermilk Pancakes (*from Pancake Palace, San Francisco*)

2 cups sifted all-purpose flour
1 teaspoon *each* soda and salt
2 tablespoons sugar
2 slightly beaten eggs
2 cups buttermilk
2 tablespoons butter, melted

Sift together dry ingredients. Add remaining ingredients; stir just till moistened. (There will be a few lumps.) Bake on hot, lightly greased griddle. (For uniform cakes, use a ¼-cup measure.) Turn cakes when bubbles on surface break. Serve with Whipped Orange Butter and syrup. Makes about 1½ dozen 4-inch cakes.

Blueberry Pancakes: Drain one 1-pound can blueberries. Add ⅔ cup drained berries to Buttermilk Pancake batter. Bake. To serve, sift confectioners' sugar over; sprinkle with remaining berries. Offer Whipped Orange Butter.

Hawaiian Pancakes: Drain one 9-ounce can crushed pineapple; fold into Buttermilk Pancake batter. Bake; top with confectioners' sugar, Whipped Orange Butter.

Tips for prize pancakes— *Pour* batter, for ease. When bubbly on top, turn cakes. To *flip*, give sudden lift-and-tilt to spatula—up and over! Keep 'em hot between layers of dish towels in warm oven.

For fun, bake crispy Orange Dessert Waffles right at the table. Top with fluffy Whipped Orange Butter for a delightful flavor treat.

Corn-meal Pancakes–ideal brunch mainliner. They're light, tender, and boast a corn-meal crunch! Partners: baked apples, sausage.

Whipped Orange Butter

Whip ½ cup softened butter until fluffy. Add ¼ teaspoon grated orange rind and 1 tablespoon confectioners' sugar; blend well. Chill mixture.

Remove whipped butter from refrigerator about 1 hour before serving.

Coconut Hot Cakes with Sausage
(*from Kona Inn, Hawaii*)

    2 cups sifted all-purpose flour
    4 teaspoons baking powder
    Dash salt
    2 beaten eggs
    2 cups milk
    ¼ cup butter, melted
            • • •
    Fresh grated or flaked coconut
    10 cooked smoked sausage links

Sift together the flour, baking powder, and salt. Combine eggs, milk, and melted butter; add mixture to dry ingredients, stirring just until the flour is moistened. (There will be a few lumps.)

Bake on a hot griddle, turning only once. Spread warm cakes with honey or coconut syrup and roll up each.

Place 3 cakes on a mound of flaked coconut for a serving; drizzle with melted butter. Top with butter pats and sizzling sausage. Pass warm maple syrup. (At the Kona Inn they offer guava jelly, papaya jam and poha jelly, too.) Makes 5 servings.

Easy Sourdough Flapjacks

Soften 1 package active dry yeast in ¼ cup *warm* water. Beat 1 egg; stir in 2 cups milk, and 2 cups packaged biscuit mix. Stir in yeast. Let stand 1 to 1½ hours. *Do not stir.* Bake on a hot, lightly greased griddle. Makes 24 4-inch flapjacks.

Orange Dessert Waffles

    1¼ cups sifted cake flour
    3 teaspoons baking powder
    ½ teaspoon salt
    2 well-beaten eggs
    1 cup light cream
    1 tablespoon grated orange rind
    ¼ cup butter, melted and
        cooled slightly
    2 stiff-beaten egg whites

Sift together dry ingredients. Combine eggs, cream, orange rind; stir into dry ingredients. Stir in butter; fold in egg whites. Bake. Serve with Whipped Orange Butter. Makes 3 10-inch waffles.

Peanut-butter Waffles

Combine 1 cup packaged pancake mix, 2 tablespoons sugar, ⅓ cup chunk-style peanut butter, 1 egg, 1 cup milk, and 2 tablespoons salad oil or melted shortening. Beat with rotary or electric beater just till almost smooth. (There will be a few lumps.) Bake in preheated baker.

To serve, pass butter, jelly, or maple-flavored syrup. Makes 8 4-inch waffles.

Index